Machine Learning For Absolute Beginners

Oliver Theobald

CONTENTS

INTRODUCTION

It's a Friday night at home and you've just placed your smartphone down on the kitchen bench after ordering a pizza. Within seconds of putting down the phone, you receive a message from your friend who wants to hang out at your house tonight. While you don't mind your friend joining you, this arrangement is less than practical.

First, your friend doesn't have a car. If your friend is to come over, you will need to drive over to his house to collect him. This normally wouldn't be a problem, as you could wait for the pizza to arrive, eat a few slices, and then leave to collect your friend from his house. But tonight that would mean missing the start of an important sports game televised live on TV. Once the match begins you won't be leaving the living room for anyone. Thus, the only available option is to collect your friend first and attempt to return back in time to receive the pizza.

You need to make a quick decision. *Do I have enough time to pick up my friend and get home before the pizza arrives?*

The pizza is estimated to arrive within 30 minutes, and if you leave now, you should have time to collect your friend and be back home within 30-35 minutes. As you know the route to your friend's house, you can safely predict the journey time with a high degree of accuracy. With this information in mind, you are willing to take a strategic gamble and hope for a positive outcome.

But as you approach the front door, a sudden realization freezes you in your tracks. The optimism that filled you a second ago begins to dissipate as a second variable now paralyzes you.

In addition to estimating the journey time to collect your friend, you are yet to predict when the pizza will arrive. There is a range of factors that could affect when your pizza arrives, including how many customers are ordering pizza tonight, whether you will have the same delivery person as last time, as well as the accuracy of the estimated delivery time made by the teenager who took your order. These three variables each have the potential to affect the pizza's time of arrival.

There are three possible methods to tackle this hypothetical dilemma. The first option is to apply direct existing knowledge. However, you don't have any previous experience ordering a pizza on a Friday night. The second option is to ask someone else. This option you've already exhausted. The squeaky-voiced teenager on the phone already told you that your pizza will arrive "within 30 minutes," and while this is a strong indication, it is not a definite prediction. The third option is to apply statistical modeling. Given that you have chosen to read a beginner's introduction to machine learning, you select the third option.

You first think back to your previous experience of ordering home delivery from Joe's Pizza on other days of the week and apply this information to predict the likelihood of the pizza arriving at your house on time. If the expected delivery time exceeds 30 minutes, you can justify your decision to collect your friend and return in time to receive and pay for the pizza.

Let's assume you have ordered pizza on eight previous occasions and the delivery time exceeded the estimated arrival time by more than ten minutes on four occasions. With a potential window of 40 minutes (30 minutes + 10 minutes late), there is approximately a 50% (4/8) chance that you will have time to collect your friend and return in time.

In order to activate a decision to leave the house, you demand a confidence level of greater than 70%. Based on previous experience, your prediction rate of 50% does not meet your confidence threshold and you consent to stay at home and figure out an excuse to decline your friend's invitation.

Basing one's decision on existing data is known as the *empirical method.* The concept of empirical data-backed decision-making is an integral component of statistical modeling and machine learning. Predictions formed through statistical modeling and machine learning depend strongly on known properties.

Predictive models in machine learning consist of at least two variables. One variable is the result you wish to predict, known as the *dependent variable (y)*. In this example, the dependent variable is whether the pizza delivery will be ≥ 10 minutes late. The second variable is the *independent variable (X)*, which again predicts whether the pizza will be late but in relation to an independent event. In our fictional scenario, 'day of the week,' could be an independent variable. Machine learning then boils down to discerning how X (the independent variable/s) affects y (the dependent variable).

Now that we have a baseline understanding of dependent and independent variables, let's return to our pizza delivery story. You recollect that on three of the four occasions you ordered from Joe's pizza on a Monday night, the pizza arrived 10 minutes later than the estimated arrival time.

Based on your previous experience, and notwithstanding the three late deliveries that occurred on a Monday, deliveries from Joe's Pizza typically arrive within the estimated time period. With this information in mind, you can create a new model to predict the probability of the pizza arriving late tonight. You decide to use a decision tree to create this simple model.

From this decision tree model, we can see there's a 75% chance the pizza will arrive later than the estimated arrival time when ordered on a Monday. This outcome contracts to 25% when ordered on another day of the week. The pizza delivery is hence three times more likely to arrive late on a Monday than any other day of the week.

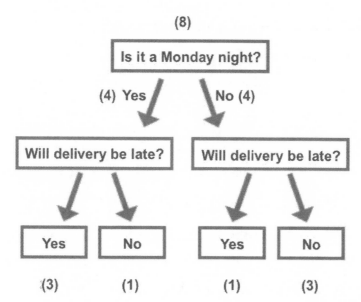

(8)

| Is it a Monday night? |

(4) Yes — No (4)

| Will delivery be late? | | Will delivery be late? |

| Yes | No | | Yes | No |

(3) (1) (1) (3)

Given that today is not a Monday, you can infer that there's a 25% chance of your pizza arriving later than the anticipated delivery time. The prediction derived from this model reinforces your decision not to leave the house and to instead wait for your pizza, which has a 75% chance of arriving within 30 minutes.

The model we created is relatively simple because there is only one independent variable. In machine learning, there are normally multiple independent variables and the model must be robust to process these additional inputs.

Let's now expand our prediction model and add 'traffic congestion' as a second independent variable. The new model now includes two independent variables in addition to the one dependent variable.

Dependent variable = Will the pizza be late by more than ten minutes?

Independent variable 1 = Is it a Monday night? (Yes/No)

Independent variable 2 = Traffic congestion (light, medium, or heavy)

We now need to predict the number of minutes the pizza will be late according to the degree of traffic congestion (light = 0 minutes, moderate = 5, heavy = 10 minutes), and the day of the week. As the route to your friend's house is unaffected by Friday night traffic, let's also assume that traffic congestion does not affect the time it takes for you to collect your friend.

A decision tree is less suitable for building this model. Decision trees are ideally used for predicting binary values (yes/no). However, with the help of other machine learning algorithms, such as regression analysis, you can attempt to create a new model to integrate these two independent variables.

It's now time to sit down at your computer. For the sake of the story, let's forget that your friend is waiting for your final response. Instead, we'll turn our attention to the topic of machine learning.

For decades, machines operated on responding to direct user commands. In other words, computers were designed to perform set tasks in response to pre-programmed commands. Now, computers don't strictly need to receive an 'input command' to perform a task but rather 'input data'. Specifically, the machine creates a predictive model based on previous experiences captured in the data. From the input of data, the machine is then able to formulate decisions on how, where and when to perform a certain action. In the case of our earlier example, the model was predicting whether the pizza delivery would be late based on existing data.

Input Command VS Input Data

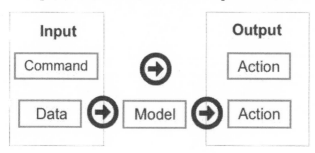

Later in the book, we will review regression analysis and other relevant machine learning algorithms that can be used to build a predictive model. In the next section, we examine background information on how machine learning relates to other relevant fields and disciplines.

## 2

FROM DATA SCIENCE TO AI, TO

MACHINE LEARNING

Data science is a broad term that encompasses a number of topics and disciplines including big data, artificial intelligence, data mining, and machine learning.

The field of studying large volumes of data, known as 'data science,' is relatively new to human history and has grown hand-in-hand with the development and wide adoption of computers. Prior to computers, data was collected and processed manually under the umbrella of 'statistics,' or what we might now refer to as 'classical statistics.'

Baseball batting averages, for example, existed long before the advent of computers. Anyone with a pencil, notepad, and basic arithmetic skills could calculate Babe Ruth's baseball batting average with the use of classical statistics. The process of calculating Ruth's batting average involved the dedication to collect and review batting sheets, and the application of basic statistics, including addition and division.

While advanced tiers of classical statistics have existed for centuries, processing capabilities and storage limitations both constricted the size of datasets available. Until recently, tabular datasets with millions of rows and columns were far outside our cognitive reach.

The evolution of computers in the 20th Century then radically transformed the field of statistics and modern computing technology provides the infrastructure to collect, store, and draw insight from massive reserves of data that was once impossible for humans to manage and analyze. From the joining marriage of technology and statistics, data science and its relevant sub-fields were born.

Artificial Intelligence

As a major sub-field of data science, artificial intelligence (AI) has been developing and evolving over a similar time period as data science. The term was coined more than sixty years ago when American computer scientist John McCarthy introduced the term at the 2nd Dartmouth Conference in 1956.

Artificial intelligence was originally described as a method for manufactured devices to simulate or even exceed the capabilities of humans at performing cognitive tasks. The definition of 'AI' in today's terms remains unchanged.

It's interesting to note, though, that 'artificial intelligence' and 'AI' tend to be treated with suspicion from outside observers. IBM, for example, have gone to great lengths to disguise AI as 'cognitive thinking' so as not to intimidate the average observer.

In 2015, my start-up worked with IBM Australia to produce a video series exploring the possibilities of 'cognitive thinking' in Asia. When we probed IBM on why we must use 'cognitive thinking' in place of 'artificial intelligence' or 'AI,' IBM referenced the negative association that has built up over the years regarding AI. In other words, they wanted us to avoid using the term 'AI' or 'artificial intelligence' because the average person on the street might associate AI with Terminator-style robots on a mission to destroy humanity!

Are the robots really going to take over the world? The portrayal of intelligent machines in Hollywood movies has not exactly helped to convince the average person otherwise. Moreover, as many informed observers rightly point out (including Stephen Hawking and Elon Musk), man has always found diabolical means to harness and abuse newfound technology. In 2014, Hawking told the BBC that, "The development of full artificial intelligence could spell the end of the human race."[1]

As an introductory course to machine learning, we won't be sliding down any rabbit holes regarding the bigger questions of AI. My focus is on getting you up to speed with the basics of machine learning and on the path to becoming a machine

---

[1] The BBC, *Stephen Hawking warns artificial intelligence could end mankind,* 2014, www.bbc.com

learning engineer or data scientist.

Machine Learning

Machine learning has existed for decades, but only in recent times has computing power and data storage caught up to make machine learning readily accessible. Computers for a long time were inept at mimicking human-specific tasks, such as reading, translating, writing, video recognition, and identifying everyday objects. However, with advances in computing power, machines have improved dramatically at identifying patterns found in massive datasets.

Not only can machines simulate certain cognitive tasks, they're also highly efficient at solving complex problems. Humans are simply not predisposed to be as reliable and efficient as computers at handling large amounts of data. The size, complexity, and speed at which big data is generated exceed our limited capabilities.

Take for instance the following dataset:

1: [0, 0]

2: [3, 6]

3: [6, 12]

4: [9, 18]

5: [12, ?]

As humans, it's not hard for us to identify the underlying pattern in this dataset. As the second number in each row is double the number to its left, we can infer that the unknown number inside the brackets on row five is '24.' In this example, we hardly need the aid of a computer to predict the unknown result.

However, what if each row was composed of much larger numbers with decimal points running into double digits? This would make it extremely difficult for anyone to quickly process and cast an accurate prediction. This task, however, is not daunting to a machine. Machines excel at solving such problems by attempting numerous possibilities to isolate large segments of data. The machine's advanced capabilities also free up our time to focus on other core business tasks.

However, machine learning is not a turnkey or an out-of-the-box solution. Upfront human input and supervision is required. So how does one program a computer to recognize patterns that exist within datasets and to conduct machine learning? As with any machine or automated production line, there needs to be a human to prepare and supervise the overall process. This is where data scientists and machine learning engineers come into the picture.

The role of data science professionals is to organize the input data and configure statistical algorithms to create a machine learning model. The *model* is a rule to predict y based on selected independent variables (X) from the dataset.

You can think of forming a model as similar to training a guide dog. Through specialized training, guide dogs learn how to respond and behave in various scenarios. For example, the dog learns to heel at a red light or to safely lead its master around obstacles. If the guide dog has been properly trained, then over time the trainer is no longer required and the dog will apply its training to various unsupervised situations. Likewise, models in machine learning can be trained to form future decisions based on previous experience.

An example of this could be a creating a model that detects spam email messages. The model is trained to block emails with suspicious subject lines and body text containing three or more flagged keywords: dear friend, free, invoice, PayPal, Viagra, casino, payment, bankruptcy, and winner.

Input Command VS Input Data

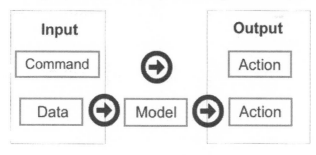

At this stage, though, we are not performing machine learning. If we return to our visual representation of *input command vs input data*, we can see that this process consists of only two steps: Command > Action.

Machine learning entails a three-step process: Data > Model > Action.

Thus, to add machine learning to our spam detection system, we need to switch out 'command' for 'data' and add 'model' in order to generate the final action. In this example, the data would comprise sample emails and the model would consist of statistical-based rules. The parameters of the model include the same keywords from our original negative list. The model is then trained and tested against the data.

Once data is fed into the model, there is a strong chance that assumptions contained in the model will lead to some inaccurate predictions. For example, under the rules of our model, the following email subject line would be automatically flagged as spam:

"**PayPal** has rejected your **payment** for **Casino** Royale purchased on eBay."

As this is a genuine email sent from a PayPal auto-responder, the spam detection system is lured into producing a false positive according to the negative list of keywords contained in the model.

Traditional programming is highly susceptible to such cases because there is no built-in mechanism to test assumptions and modify rules. Machine learning, on the other hand, can adapt and modify assumptions through its three-step process and ability to respond to prediction error.

In machine learning, data is split into *training data* and *test data*.

The first split of the data provides the training data. This is the initial data you will use to develop your model. In the case of our spam detection example, false positives similar to the PayPal example might be detected with the training data. New rules or modifications are then added, i.e. email notifications issued from the sending address payments@paypal.com are automatically excluded from spam filtering.

After you have successfully developed a model based on the training data and are satisfied with its accuracy, you can test the model on the remaining data, known as the test data. Then, once you are satisfied with the results of both the training and test data, your machine learning model is ready for use; to filter incoming emails and generate decisions on which email messages to accept and block.

In this example, we (as the machine learning engineer) dictated which keywords (rules) would activate the spam filter. However, it is also possible for machines to develop their only rules to define a predictive model through what is known as self-learning, as covered in the subsequent chapter.

## 3

SELF-LEARNING

A crucial component of machine learning is the usage of self-improving algorithms and techniques. Just as humans learn from previous experiences and trial and error to formulate decisions, so too can machines.

In the previous chapter, you were introduced to an example of an email spam filter that could detect suspicious email messages based on a negative list of keywords. Keywords are easy to define, and in general, can be applied with relatively high accuracy. But what if we wish to program a computer to perform more complex tasks, such as image recognition, void of any upfront instructions? How can a computer be programmed to recognize subtle physical differences between certain animal groups?

The machine learning engineer, of course, cannot program the computer to recognize animals based on instructions and a general description (i.e. four legs, long tail and long neck), as this would induce a high rate of error. This is because there are countless combinations of animals with similar characteristics. Solving such complex tasks has long been the limitation of computers and traditional computer programming. Instead, we must train the machine to identify animals following a similar methodology that parents use to teach children to perform the same task.

Young children are unlikely to recognize a 'goat' based on the mere description of key features. An animal with four legs, white fur, and a short neck, for instance, could naturally be confused with various other animals. Rather than playing a guessing game with the child, a more effective approach is to demonstrate the visual and physical attributes of a goat through presenting multiple examples to the child, such as toys, images, or even real-life examples of a goat grazing in a paddock.

Image recognition in machine learning utilizes a similar methodology, except that teaching is managed via images (input data) and a programming language to develop a model. This process starts with feeding images to the machine labeled as the subject, i.e. 'goat.' The machine then draws on these examples to design a model that analyzes patterns and identifies common features. The model is then used to identify future instances of the subject.

Whether it's recognizing animals, human faces or even illicit material, the machine relies on data and experience to develop a self-learning model. This eliminates the need for humans to provide an in-depth description of each subject matter and improves the overall accuracy of classification.

The model can also be modified in response to changes in the data. If goats are genetically modified and adopt previously unseen features, such as a change in color, the model will inevitably incur error with its classification. However, at any time, the machine learning model can be retrained with new data to modify and update its model. Alternatively, training can be ongoing and not just conducted at fixed intervals. Reinforcement learning is used for this explicit purpose: to automatically adjust the model according to new input data. We will discuss reinforcement learning later in this book.

Another example of self-learning is Google's new search engine technology. Prior to the integration of advanced machine learning, Google focused its search service heavily around strings of letters where they indexed millions of web pages each day to track content for strings of letters. This included strings found in a web page's title, navigation menu, body text, meta tags, image descriptions, and so on. With these string combinations stored in a massive repository, Google could generate results based on the string you queried. If you typed in "Donald Trump," the search engine would connect to its repository and return web pages with that exact string:

d-o-n-a-l-d t-r-u-m-p

While there are various factors that influence search rankings, including backlinks and page speed, string letter matching has traditionally played a pivotal role in Google's page ranking algorithm. Web pages containing the exact string of letters entered by the user would thus feature prominently on the first page of the search results.

But Google's new algorithm—backed by machine learning—treats "Donald Trump" not just as a string of letters but as an actual person. A person who has a defined age, a defined job profile, a list of relatives, a list of wives, and so on. As a result, Google can better decipher the relevance of content in regards to your search query without solely relying on matching strings of letters.

Let's say you want to search: "Who was Donald Trump's first wife?"

Prior to machine learning, Google would search for web pages containing those six exact keywords as strings of letters. However, the accuracy of the results was prone to error. By mistake, the search engine might return a number of web pages that were less relevant but contained similar strings of letters, such as:

"Melania Trump: **Donald Trump's wife** and the **First** Lady of the United States of America."

From your original search request, Google would thereby be lured into returning content featuring Melania Trump (Trump's third wife) on the first page of its search results. The same error still happens in the year 2017 if you search on Yahoo.

who was donald trump's first wife

Donald and Ivana Trump's Divorce: The Full Story | Vanity Fair
www.vanityfair.com/magazine/2015/07/donald-ivana-trump... ⌄
Unfortunately for **Donald** and Ivana **Trump**, ... I thought about the ten years since I had **first** met
Donald Trump. ... The Most Fabulous Yachts at Sea BY VANITY FAIR. SEEK.

Why Ivana Trump, Donald Trump's Ex-Wife, Prefers To Date ...
www.huffingtonpost.com/...trump-boyfriends-donald-trump_n... ⌄
Dec 22, 2013 · **Donald Trump's** ex-**wife** Ivana **Trump** ... "Me and **Donald** are very friendly, ... "The
Huffington Post" is a registered trademark of TheHuffingtonPost.com, Inc.

Donald Trump's Ex-Wife Ivana Disavows Old 'Rape' Allegation ...
abcnews.go.com/Politics/donald-trumps-wife-ivana...
Jul 27, 2015 · **Donald Trump's** Ex-**Wife** Ivana Disavows Old 'Rape' Allegation. ... **Donald Trump's**
first wife, ... The Many Lives of **Donald** J. **Trump**." ...

Trump's wife Melania Knauss-Trump a first lady of fashion ...
www.nydailynews.com/life-style/fashion/donald-trump-wife...
The **Donald's** better half could **trump** every other First Lady. .. **Donald Trump's wife** Melania
Knauss-**Trump** a ... The **Donald's** better half could **trump** every other ...

Melania Trump - Wikipedia
en.wikipedia.org/wiki/Melania_Trump ⌄
... **wife** of **Donald Trump** and First Lady of the United States. ... Melania **Trump** (born Melanija
Knavs ... **Donald** described their long courtship in 2005: ...

Ivana Trump - Model, Writer, Television Personality ...
www.biography.com/people/ivana-trump-9542158 ⌄
Synopsis. Ivana **Trump** is a former model and **wife** of **Donald Trump** who was born in Gottwaldov
(now Zlín), Czechoslovakia (now the Czech Republic), in 1949.

Source: Yahoo Search

Today, Google boasts more accurate results courtesy of machine
learning. As mentioned, Google is able to decipher words not just
as strings of letters, but as 'things,' things that have learnt
relationships with other things.

who was donald trump's first wife 🎤 🔍

All   News   Images   Shopping   Videos   More   Settings   Tools

Donald Trump › **Ex-spouses**

Ivana Trump		Marla Maples	
1977 – 1992		1993 – 1999	

Donald Trump's first wife reveals what to expect from his presidency: 'I ...
www.independent.co.uk › News › People ▾
Nov 14, 2016 - While many are busy speculating about what the next four years with **Donald Trump** as President will look like, **Ivana Trump** has actually given ...

Donald Trump's family tree: Melania, Ivanka, Tiffany, Eric and more ...
www.amny.com/.../**donald**-trump-s-**family**-tree-melania-ivanka-tiffany-eric-and-more... ▾
Jan 20, 2017 - Donald Trump Jr., son. Donald Trump Jr., 39, is Donald Trump's oldest child with **Ivana Trump**. He serves as an executive vice president of the Trump Organization. Donald Jr. is married to Vanessa Haydon and they have five children.

Ivana Trump - Wikipedia
https://en.wikipedia.org/wiki/Ivana_Trump ▾
Ivana Marie Trump is a Czech-born American businesswoman, author, socialite, and former fashion model. She was the **first wife** of **Donald Trump**. ... In October 1990, **Ivana Trump's** 63-year-old father died suddenly from a heart attack. ... Three years after her **divorce** from **Donald**, Ivana married **Riccardo Mazzucchelli**.

Source: Google Search

With the aid of machine learning, Google is immediately aware that the search query "who is Donald Trump's first wife?" relates to "Ivana Trump" and not "Melania Trump." Google is aware of this relationship based on analysis and insight gained from past search queries. Similar search queries from users likely link to a very high click-through rate to content that contains the keywords "Ivana Trump." From users' past search activities and the links they click on, Google is able to log a relationship between the keywords "Donald Trump's first wife" and "Ivana Trump." Given that Google understands Ivana Trump to be Donald Trump's first wife, it can eliminate all other content not concerning Ivana Trump from its top results. As Wired Magazine Founding Executive Editor Kevin Kelly explains, "Each of the three billion queries that Google conducts each day tutors the Google AI over and over again."[2]

But what's even more exciting is Google's new ability to understand interconnected search queries. For example, let's now search using a string that doesn't directly refer to Donald Trump. "Who was his second wife?"

This string is extremely broad and unspecific. However, given that the search engine has already processed our first search query referencing "Donald Trump," Google can easily decipher the subject of our second search query. Google returns results concerning Donald Trump's second wife, Marla Maples. Google is able to achieve this feat with no direct reference to relevant strings, such as "Donald Trump" and "Marla Maples."

Google's new line of advanced reasoning and self-learning resembles human behavior, and which is why Google's new technology falls squarely under the banner of artificial intelligence and machine learning.

---

[2] Kevin Kelly, *The Inevitable: Understanding the 12 Technological Forces That Will Shape Our Future*, Penguin Books, 2016.

Google's focus on machine learning and AI, including the acquisition of Deepmind in 2014, will surface prominently as you proceed further in your study on this subject.

Part of Google's current and future dominance in self-learning algorithms lies in their access to training data. In his 2016 novel, *The Inevitable: Understanding the 12 Technological Forces That Will Shape Our Future*, Kevin Kelly dispels Google's recent acquisition of thirteen AI companies (in addition to Deepmind) as buying its way to the top of the AI leaderboard.

Referencing the recent acquisitions, Kelly explains that, "At first glance, you might think that Google is beefing up its AI portfolio to improve its search capabilities...but I think that's backward. Rather than use AI to make its search better, Google is using search to make its AI better."[3]

---

[3] Kevin Kelly, *The Inevitable: Understanding the 12 Technological Forces That Will Shape Our Future*, Penguin Books, 2016.

## 4

TOOLS

Computer programming is an essential skill for budding machine learning engineers and data scientists. While machine learning is likely to venture in the same direction as web development with click-and-drag software (think WordPress and Wix), computer programming is imperative for anyone wishing to dabble in machine learning today.

To maximize computing performance, C and C++ are go-to languages for machine learning. However, Python remains the preferred programming language for most machine learning professionals, as you will soon find out.

Machine learning demands high levels of computational power. For large datasets, machine learning algorithms are best performed on a GPU (graphical processing unit), rather than a CPU. The GPU is able to perform many more floating point operations per second than the CPU, allowing you to solve problems in linear algebra and statistics much faster than with the CPU alone. C and C++ are the preferred languages to directly edit and perform mathematical operations on the GPU. However, Python can also be used and converted into C when used in combination with TensorFlow from Google.

As the most popular machine learning framework, TensorFlow supports neural networks, calculus, reinforcement learning, and various other machine learning algorithms. It's possible to run TensorFlow on the CPU, but for advanced machine learning, you should look at investing in a GPU cluster from AWS (Amazon Web Services) or an equivalent cloud provider as you proceed to build more complex models.

Other relevant programming languages to machine learning include R, MATLAB, and Octave. R is a free and open-source programming language optimized for mathematical operations, and conducive to building matrices and statistical functions, which are built directly into the language libraries of R. Although R is commonly used for data analytics and data mining, R also supports machine learning operations as well.

MATLAB and Octave are direct competitors to R. MATLAB is a commercial and propriety programming language. It is strong in regards to solving algebraic equations and is also a quick programming language to learn. MATLAB is widely used in electrical engineering, chemical engineering, civil engineering, and aeronautical engineering. However, computer scientists and computer engineers tend not to rely on MATLAB as heavily. In machine learning, MATLAB is more often used in academia than in industry. Thus, while you may see MATLAB featured in online courses, and especially on Coursera, this is not to say that it's commonly used in the wild. If, however, you're coming from an engineering background, MATLAB is certainly a logical choice.

Next, we have Octave. Octave is essentially a free version of MATLAB developed in response to MATLAB by the open-source community.

As alluded to earlier, Python remains the overwhelming first choice as the default programming language for machine learning. The disadvantage of C and C++ is they are difficult programming languages to write, and consume many more lines of code than other languages (such as Python) to achieve the same desired outcome.

Python, on the other hand, is easier to learn and operate, and can be used more widely, including data collection (web scraping) and data piping (Hadoop and Spark). Through TensorFlow, Python can then convert your code to C, which allows you to run your code on the GPU. Finally, Python offers access to a number of important machine learning libraries, including NumPy, Scikit-learn, and Pandas. These libraries provide important code templates and manipulation techniques to perform machine learning tasks in Python.

NumPy is open-source and is Python's answer to MATLAB, which allows you to manage matrices and work with large datasets. Scikit-learn provides access to a range of popular shallow machine learning algorithms, including linear regression and support vector machine. Pandas enables data to be represented on a virtual spreadsheet that you can manipulate directly from your code. The naming comes from the term 'panel data', which refers to its ability to create a series of panels, similar to sheets in an Excel spreadsheet.

NumPy, Scikit-learn, and Pandas can all be used simultaneously. Users can thereby draw on these three libraries to: load their data via NumPy, clean up and perform calculations with Pandas, and run machine learning algorithms with Scikit-learn.

MACHINE LEARNING TECHNIQUES

## 5

INTRODUCTION

There are hundreds of statistical-based algorithms to choose from in machine learning. Popular algorithms include *k*-means clustering, association analysis, and neural networks. We will examine a number of these algorithms later in this book. Let us first start by taking a look at the three overarching algorithm categories of machine learning.

Supervised Learning

Supervised learning refers to algorithms guided by pre-existing patterns and feedback based on known outcomes. In practice, supervised learning works by showing data to the machine including the correct value (output) of the data. The machine then applies a supervised learning algorithm to decipher patterns that exist in the data and develops a model that can reproduce matching results with new data.

As an example, suppose you wish to separate SMS messages into spam and non-spam clusters. In a supervised learning environment, you already have data that you can feed the machine to describe both categories. The machine understands the characteristics of both spam and non-spam messages and will sort incoming messages into these two categories based on known outcomes.

Or to predict who will win a basketball game, you might create a model to analyze previous games over the last three years. The games could be analyzed by the total number of points scored and points conceded and these scores can then be used to predict who will win the next game.

This data can be plotted on a scatterplot, with 'points for' represented on the x-axis and 'points against' represented on the y-axis. Each data point represents an individual game, and the score for each game can be found by looking up the x and y coordinates.

Linear regression (which we will learn in detail very soon) can next be applied to predict the expected winner based on the average of previous performances. As with the first example, we have instructed the machine which categories to analyze (points for, and points conceded). The data is therefore already pre-tagged, and we know the final outcome of the existing data. Each previous game has a final outcome in the form of the match score.

The challenge of supervised algorithms is having sufficient data that is representative of all variations. The data should also be relevant and if taken from a larger dataset should be selected at random to avoid any bias.

Supervised learning algorithms include regression analysis, decision trees, k-nearest neighbors, neural networks, and support vector machine.

Unsupervised Learning

In the case of an unsupervised learning environment, there are no such known patterns from which to base your analysis on. Instead, the model must uncover hidden patterns through the use of unsupervised learning algorithms.

A commonly used algorithm is k-means clustering. This algorithm creates discrete groups of data points that are found to possess similar features.

For example, if you cluster data points based on the weight and height of sixteen-year-old high school students, you are likely to see two clusters emerge. One large cluster will be male and the other large cluster will be female. This is because girls and boys tend to have noticeable differences in relation to weight and height.

A major advantage of unsupervised learning is that it enables you to discover patterns in the data that you weren't aware existed—such as the presence of two genders. Clustering or another unsupervised learning technique can then provide the springboard to conduct further analysis after particular groups have been discovered.

Unsupervised learning algorithms include *k*-means clustering, association analysis, social network analysis, and descending dimension algorithms.

Reinforcement Learning

Reinforcement learning is the third and most advanced algorithm category in machine learning. Unlike supervised and unsupervised learning, reinforcement learning continuously improves its model by leveraging feedback from previous iterations. This differs in comparison to supervised and unsupervised learning, which both reach an indefinite endpoint after the model is formulated.

Reinforcement learning is best explained through analogies to video games. As a player progresses through the virtual space of the game, they learn the value of various actions under different conditions and become more familiar with the field of play. Those learned values then inform and influence the gamer's future behavior.

Reinforcement learning is very similar. Algorithms are set to train the model through continuous learning. A standard reinforcement learning model will have measurable performance criteria where outputs are not tagged—instead, they are graded. In the case of self-driving vehicles, avoiding a crash will receive a positive score. In the case of chess, avoiding defeat will receive a positive score.

A popular algorithm for reinforcement learning is Q-learning.

With Q-learning, you start with a set environment of *states*. In Pac-Man, for instance, states could be the challenges, obstacles or pathways that exist in the game. A wall might exist to the left, a ghost to the right, and a power pill above—each representing different *states*. States are represented in Q-learning by the symbol 'S.'

The set of possible actions to respond to these states is then referred to as 'A.' In the case of Pac-Man, actions are limited to left, right, up, and down movements, as well as multiple combinations thereof.

The third important symbol is 'Q.' Q is your starting value and which has an initial value of 0.

As Pac-Man explores the space inside the game, two main things will happen:

- Q drops as negative things occur after a given state/action

- Q increases as rewards happen after a given state/action

In Q-learning, the machine will learn to match the action for a given state that generates or maintains the highest level of Q. It will learn initially through the process of random movements (actions) under different conditions (states). The machine will record its results (rewards and penalties) and how they impact its Q level, and store those values to inform and optimize its future actions.

While this sounds simple enough, implementation is a much more difficult task and beyond the scope of a beginner's introduction to machine learning. However, I will leave you with a link to a more comprehensive explanation of reinforcement learning and Q-learning following the Pac-Man scenario.

https://inst.eecs.berkeley.edu/~cs188/sp12/projects/reinforcement/rein forcement.html

## 6

MACHINE LEARNING IN ACTION

The application of machine learning can be divided into five core steps:

1) Prepare data for analysis through the process of **scrubbing**.

2) Split data into **training** and **test data**.

3) Nominate suitable **algorithms** to analyze the data.

4) Configure and modify algorithm **hyperparameters**.

5) Develop a **model** that accurately predicts training and test data.

This chapter will briefly walk you through these five steps before taking a look at specific algorithms.

First, *scrubbing* is the process of refining your dataset into a state that is manageable, accurate and relevant. This involves modifying or removing incomplete, irrelevant or duplicated data. It may also entail converting text-based data to numerical values and the redesigning of dataset features. For data scientists, data scrubbing often demands the greatest application of time and effort.

Once you have scrubbed your dataset for accuracy and relevance, your next job is to split the data into training and test sets. The ratio of the two splits should be approximately 70/30 or 80/20. This means that your training data should account for 70-80% of rows in your dataset and your test data should account for the other 20-30% of rows. It is vital to split your data by rows and not columns (variables) and to randomize the rows. This helps to avoid bias in your model, in case your original dataset is arranged in ascending or descending order depending on the time of collection. Unless you randomize your data, you may accidentally omit important variance from your training data. This will cause unnecessary surprises when you apply your model to the test data.

After randomizing the data, you next need to select algorithms to design your model based on the training data. We will cover specific algorithms used in machine learning in the coming chapters. The remaining 20-30% of data is put to the side and reserved for testing the accuracy of the model.

Using the training data, machine learning algorithms are applied and optimized to deliver optimal results to develop a model. The final step is to then measure how well the model actually performs. You will know if your model is accurate when the error rate between the training and test dataset is low. This means that the model has learned and understood the underlying patterns and trends found in the data.

Once your model can accurately predict the values of your test data, the model is ready to use in the wild. Should the model fail to accurately predict outcomes from the test data, you may need to re-randomize the data, alter the model's hyperparameters or switch to an alternative algorithm technique in order to optimize the model and reduce prediction error.

Please note that I include equations in the following chapters out of necessity, and I have kept them as simple as possible. Many of the machine learning techniques we discuss in this book already have working implementations in your programming language of choice: no equation writing necessary.

## 7

REGRESSION ANALYSIS

As the 'Hello World' of machine learning algorithms, regression analysis is a simple supervised learning technique used to find the best trendline to describe a dataset. Regression analysis is easy to understand and is very important as it provides the basis for more advanced machine learning techniques including neural networks.

Outside of machine learning, regression is used in a range of disciplines including data mining, finance, business, and investing. In investing and finance, regression is used to value assets and understand the relationship between variables such as exchange rates and commodity prices. But in a nutshell, you can see regression analysis everywhere! Regression is seen on charts to predict sales for a company, trends in social media, GDP growth, inbound tourist numbers, and so on.

Let's examine a specific example of regression analysis in the form of linear regression.

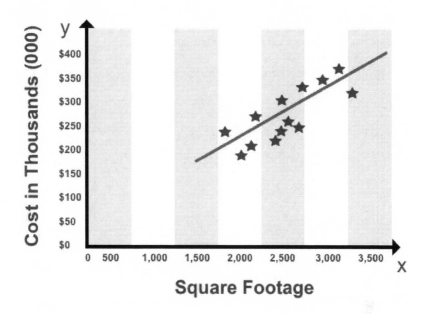

On this scatterplot, we see two quantitative variables marked as **house cost in thousands** and **square footage**. House cost is measured on the vertical axis (y) and square footage is expressed along the horizontal axis (x). Each data point represents one paired measurement of 'square footage' and 'house cost.'

As you can see on the scatterplot, there are 13 data points, each representing an individual property. We can discern the cost and square footage of each property by referencing the x and y coordinates on the scatterplot.

In order to visualize and analyze the underlying relationship between a house's value (y, dependent variable) and square footage (X, independent variable), we can apply linear regression to draw a straight line through the data points as shown on the plot. But where to draw that line? There are many potential ways we could split the data points with such a line.

In linear regression, the goal is to draw a straight line that best fits all the points on the graph, with the minimum distance possible from each point to the regression line. This means that if you were to draw a perpendicular line (a straight line at an angle of 90 degrees) from the regression line to every data point on the scatterplot, the distance of each point would equate to the smallest possible distance of any potential regression line. As you can see also, the linear regression line is straight ('linear'). If the line were not straight, it would represent a case of non-linear regression.

Another important feature of regression is *slope*, which can be calculated by referencing the regression line, known also as the hyperplane. As one variable (x or y) increases, the other variable increases or decreases to the average value denoted by the hyperplane. The slope is therefore very useful in forming predictions. The closer the data points are to the hyperplane, the more accurate the prediction. If there is a strong deviation in the distance between the data points and the hyperplane, then the slope is less accurate in its predictive ability.

How to Calculate Linear Regression

For those who wish to learn the mathematical underpinning of linear regression, I have included the following practical example.

In the next table we have the cost of individual keywords available for purchase on Google AdWords and total clicks per day. In the second column is the cost per click (CPC) of individual keywords (x) and in the third column is the total amount of clicks per day (y).

	x	y	xy	x^2
1	2.3	89	204.7	5.29
2	2.1	63	132.3	4.41
3	2.5	71	177.5	6.25
4	4.5	70	315	20.25
5	5.9	80	472	34.81
6	4.1	89	364.9	16.81
7	8.9	150	1335	79.21
Σ (Total)	30.3	612	3001.4	167.03

The fourth column calculates the value of x multiplied by the value of y for each row.

The fifth column calculates the value of x squared for each row.

To complete this equation, we only need the data available in the bottom row of each column, which represents the total of each column (Σ = Total sum).

$$a = \frac{(\Sigma y)(\Sigma x^2) - (\Sigma x)(\Sigma xy)}{n(\Sigma x^2) - (\Sigma x)^2}$$

$$b = \frac{n(\Sigma xy) - (\Sigma x)(\Sigma y)}{n(\Sigma x^2) - (\Sigma x)^2}$$

This equation may look daunting at first, but I can assure you, it's easy once you understand the algebraic expressions.

First, "Σ" equals sum. So Σxy is the total sum of x multiplied by y. Also, '**n**' equals the total number of sample items, which in our particular example is 7. Let's now complete the equation by plugging in the values from the table.

STEP 1

Find the value of a:

- $((612 \times 167.03) - (30.3 \times 3{,}001.4)) / (7(167.03) - 30.3^2)$
- $(102{,}222.36 - 90{,}942.42) / (1{,}169.21 - 918.09)$
- $11{,}279.94 / 251.12$

  = **44.919**

STEP 2

Find the value of b:

- $(7(3001.4) - (30.3 \times 612)) / (7(167.03) - 30.3^2)$
- $(21{,}009.8 - 18{,}543.6) / (1{,}169.21 - 918.09)$
- $2466.2 / 251.12$

= **9.821**

STEP 3

Insert the 'a' and 'b' values into a linear equation.

y = a + bx

y = 44.919 + 9.821x

Please note that **a** and **b** are rounded to three decimal places.

The linear equation y = 44.919 + 9.821x describes how to draw our regression line.

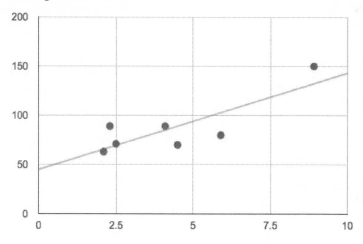

Multi-linear Regression

Multi-linear (non-linear) regression is similar to linear regression in that it seeks to track a particular response from a set of variables on the scatterplot. However, rather than drawing a straight line through the data, multi-linear regression draws a non-linear line between data points to best fit the data.

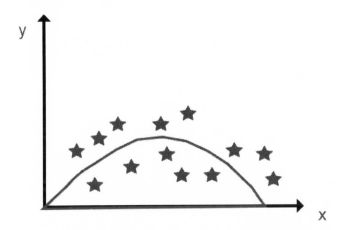

Multi-linear regression models are somewhat more complicated to develop, but they can be created through a series of approximations (iterations), typically based on a system of trial and error. The Gauss-Newton method and the Levenberg-Marquardt method are popular non-linear regression modeling techniques.

Logistic Regression

A large part of data analysis boils down to a simple question: is something 'A' or 'B?' Is it 'positive' or 'negative?' Is this person a 'potential customer' or 'not a potential customer?' Machine learning accommodates such questions through logistic equations, and specifically through what is known as the *sigmoid function*. The sigmoid function produces an S-shaped curve that can convert any number and map it into a numerical value between 0 and 1 but without ever reaching those exact limits.

A common application of the sigmoid function is found in logistic regression. Logistic regression adopts the sigmoid function to analyze data and predict discrete classes that exist in a dataset. Although logistic regression shares a visual resemblance to linear regression, it is actually a classification technique. Whereas linear regression addresses numerical equations and forms numerical predictions to discern relationships between variables, logistic regression predicts discrete classes.

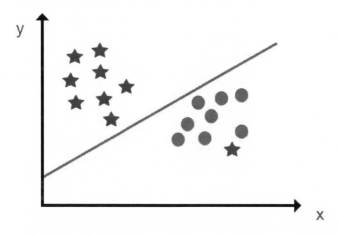

Logistic regression is typically used for binary classification to predict two discrete classes, i.e. *pregnant* or *not pregnant*. To do this, the sigmoid function is added to compute the result and convert numerical results into an expression of probability between 0 and 1.

$$y = \frac{1}{1+e^{-x}}$$

The logistic sigmoid function is calculated as '1' divided by '1' plus 'e' raised to the power of minus 'x', where:

x = the numerical value you wish to transform

e = Euler's constant, 2.718

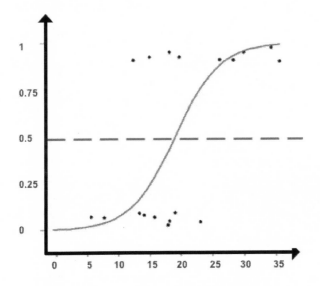

In a binary case, a value of 0 represents no chance of occurring, and 1 represents a certain chance of occurring. The degree of probability for values located between 0 and 1 can be calculated according to how close they rest to 0 (impossible) or 1 (certain possibility).

Based on the found probabilities we can assign two discrete classes. As seen in the diagram, we can create a cut-off point at 0.5 to classify data points into these two classes. Anything above 0.5 is classified as class A, and anything below 0.5 is classified as class B. Data points that record a result of exactly 0.5 are unclassifiable, but such instances are rare due to the

50

mathematical component of the sigmoid function.

Given its strength in binary classification, logistic regression is commonly used in fraud detection, disease diagnosis, emergency detection, loan default detection, or to identify spam email through the process of identifying specific classes, i.e. non-spam and spam. However, logistic regression can also be applied to ordinal cases where there are a set number of discrete values, i.e. single, married, and divorced. Logistic regression with more than two outcome values is known as multinomial logistic regression (as seen in the diagram).

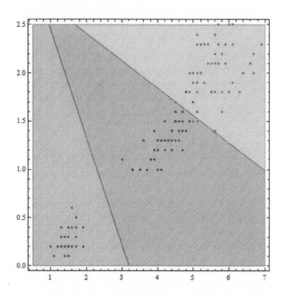

Two tips to remember when performing logistic regression are that the data should be free of missing values and that all variables are independent of each other. There should also be sufficient data for each outcome value so as to ensure accuracy. A good starting point would be approximately 30-50 data points for each outcome, i.e. 60-100 total data points for binary cases.

## 8

CLUSTERING ANALYSIS

One helpful approach to analyze data is to identify clusters of data that share similar attributes. For example, your company may wish to examine a segment of customers that purchase at the same time of year and discern what factors influence their purchasing behavior.

By understanding a particular cluster of customers, you can then form decisions on which products to recommend through promotions and specialized offers. Outside of market research, clustering can also be applied to various other scenarios, including pattern recognition and image processing.

Clustering analysis falls under the banner of both supervised and unsupervised learning. As a supervised learning technique, clustering can be utilized to classify new data points into existing clusters through k-nearest neighbors (k-NN). As an unsupervised learning algorithm, clustering can be applied to identify discrete groups of data points with k-means clustering.

k-Nearest Neighbors

The simplest clustering algorithm is *k*-nearest neighbors (*k*-NN), a supervised learning technique used to classify new data points based on the relationship to known and nearby data points. As this technique is simple to learn, we can proceed directly to a visual example.

Imagine a scatterplot that has been categorized into two known classes (circles and stars).

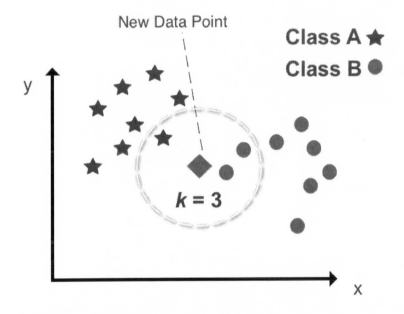

A new data point (a diamond), whose category is unknown, is then added to the scatterplot. It is now our task to predict the category of the new data point based on its relationship with other nearby data points (neighbors).

First, though, we must set '*k*' to determine how many nearby data points we wish to select in order to classify the unknown data point. If we set k to '3', k-NN will only analyze the three closest data points. If we set k to '5', k-NN will analyze the five closest data points. Setting k to '3' selects the three closest neighbors and returns two Class B data points (circles) and one Class A data point (star). Based on the three closest neighbors, the model predicts that the unknown data point likely belongs to Class B.

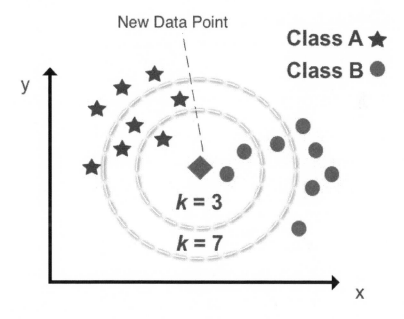

The selection of sample data, defined by k, is crucial in determining the results. In the second scatterplot, we can see that classification varies between k '3' and k '7'.

k '3' = Class A (1), **Class B (2)**

k '7' = **Class A (4)**, Class B (3)

It is therefore recommended that you test numerous k combinations to find the best fit, and avoid setting k too high or too low.

Another potential downside of *k*-NN is that it can be computationally expensive to run, especially for large datasets. For *k*-NN to operate effectively, it requires significant computational resources to store an entire dataset and to calculate the distance between all data points. This algorithm is generally not recommended for sorting large datasets, but do watch this space, as tech companies are sponsoring research to 'prune' datasets in order to streamline *k*-NN classification.

Another drawback is that it can be challenging to apply *k*-NN to high-dimensional data (3-D and 4-D) with numerous features. Measuring the multiple distances between data points in a three or four-dimensional space is again taxing on computing resources and complicated when trying to perform accurate classification. Reducing the total number of dimensions, through a data reduction technique such as Principle Component Analysis or merging variables, is a common strategy to simplify and prepare a dataset for *k*-NN analysis.

k-Means Clustering

Another popular clustering technique commonly used in machine learning is *k*-means clustering. Contrary to *k*-NN, *k*-means is an unsupervised learning algorithm and does not rely on known classes to classify new data points. It is used to identify and then create clusters based on similar attributes among groupings of data points.

In practice, *k*-means clustering attempts to split data into *k* groups/clusters, where *k* represents the number of groups that you wish to define. Setting *k* to '3' will thereby split your data into three groups. Each group is then assigned a **centroid**, which is a data point that determines the central location of the entire group.

Below is a practical example of *k*-means clustering. The dataset for this example is comprised of seven bottles of beer (each a different brand) along with two variables: wholesale price and retail price. In this example, *k* is set to '2' and will thus attempt to split the dataset into two clusters.

Bottle	Cost Price ($)	Retail Price ($)
A	1	2
B	3	5
C	5	6
D	5	7
E	2.5	3.5
F	5	8
G	3	4

Step 1: Let's first visualize this dataset on a scatterplot.

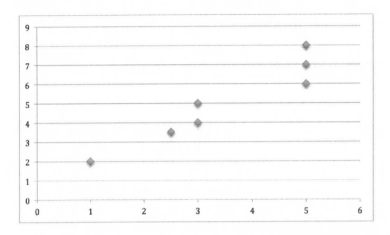

Each data point on the scatterplot represents one beer bottle, with the horizontal x-axis representing wholesale price and the y-axis representing retail price.

Step 2: With k set to '2', the next step is to split the data into two clusters. To create two clusters, we nominate two data points to act as centroids. You can think of a centroid as a team leader. Other data points then report to the closest centroid according to their location on the scatterplot.

Centroids can be chosen at random, and in this example we have nominated data points A (1, 2) and D (5, 7) to act as our two centroids. The two centroids are now represented as circles on the scatterplot.

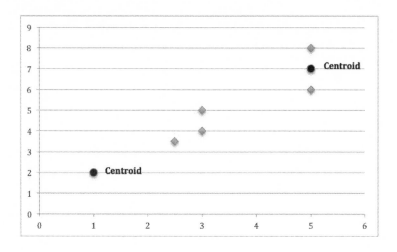

Step 3: The remaining data points are assigned to the closest centroid, as summarized in the following table.

Cluster 1		Cluster 2	
Bottle	**Mean Value**	**Bottle**	**Mean Value**
A* (1.0, 2.0)	(1.0, 2.0)	D* (5.0, 7.0)	(5.0, 7.0)
		B (3.0, 5.0)	(4.0, 6.0)
		C (5.0, 6.0)	(4.33, 6.0)
E (2.5, 3.5)	(1.75, 2.75)		
		F (5.0, 8.0)	(4.5, 6.5)
G (3.0, 4.0)	(2.16, 3.2)		
A, E, G	**(2.16, 3.2)**	**D, B, C, F**	**(4.5, 6.5)**

* Centroid

Cluster 1 comprises data points A, E, G, and together their mean value is **2.16**, **3.2**. Cluster 2 comprises data points B, C, D, F, and together their mean value is **4.5**, **6.5**. The two clusters and their respective centroid (A and D) are visualized in the next scatterplot.

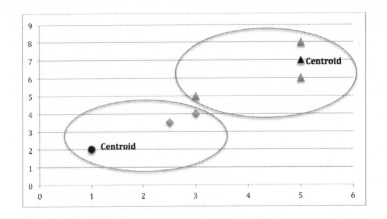

Step 4: We now use the mean value, calculated at the previous step, to update our two centroids' location. The new centroid location for Cluster 1 is **2.16**, **3.2**. The new centroid location for Cluster 2 is **4.5**, **6.5**.

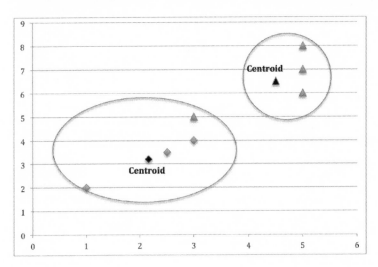

Step 5: Next, we need to check that each data point remains aligned with its updated centroid. Immediately we see that one

data point has switched sides and joined the opposite cluster! That data point is B (3, 5).

We thus need to go back and update the mean value of each cluster, with data point B now assigned as a group member of Cluster 1, rather than Cluster 2.

Cluster 1			Cluster 2		
	X Value	Y Value		X Value	Y Value
A	1	2	C	5	6
B	3	5	D	5	7
E	2.5	3.5	F	5	8
G	3	4			
Mean	2.4	3.5	Mean	5	7

Cluster 1 now comprises data points A, B, E, G. The updated centroid is **2.4, 3.5**. Cluster 2 now comprises data points C, D, F. The updated centroid is **5.0, 7.0**.

Step 6: Let's now plug in our updated centroids on the scatterplot. You may notice that we are missing a data point. This is because the new centroid for Cluster 2 overlaps with data point D (5, 7), but this does not mean it has been removed or forgotten.

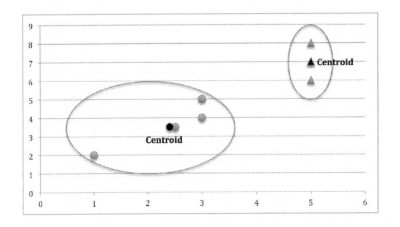

In this iteration, each individual data point remains closest to its original cluster centroid, and no data point has switched clusters. This provides us with our final result. Cluster 1 is A, B, E, G, and Cluster 2 is C, D, F.

For this example, it took two iterations to successfully create our two clusters. However, k-means clustering is not always able to reliably identify a final combination of clusters. In which case you will need to switch tactics and utilize another algorithmic approach to formulate your classification model.

Setting k

It is important to strike a balance regarding the number of k clusters you create. In general, as k increases, clusters become smaller and variance falls. However, the downside is that neighboring clusters become less distinct from one other as k increases.

If you set k to the same number of data points found in your dataset, each data point automatically becomes a standalone cluster. Conversely, if you set *k* to 1, then all data points will be deemed as homogenous and produce only one cluster. Needless to say, setting *k* at either extreme does not provide any worthy new insight for analysis.

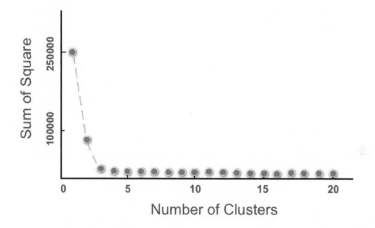

In order to optimize *k*, you may wish to turn to a scree plot for guidance. A scree plot charts the degree of scatter (variance) inside a cluster as the total number of clusters increases. Scree plots are famous for their iconic 'elbow,' which reflects several pronounced kinks in the plot's curve.

A scree plot compares the Sum of Squared Error (SSE) for each variation of clusters. SSE is measured as the sum of the squared distance between the centroid and the other neighbors inside the cluster. In a nutshell, SSE drops as more clusters are added.

This then raises the question of what the optimal number of clusters is. In general, you should opt for a cluster solution where SSE subsides dramatically to its left on the scree plot, but before it reaches a point of negligible change with cluster variations to its right.

For instance, in the diagram, there is little impact on SSE for 6 or more clusters. This would result in clusters that would be small and difficult to distinguish.

In this scree plot, 2 or 3 clusters appear to be an ideal solution. There exists a significant kink to the left of these two cluster variations due to a pronounced drop-off in SSE. Meanwhile, there is still some change in SSE with the solution to their right. This will ensure that these two cluster solutions are distinct and have an impact on data classification.

9

DIMENSIONALITY REDUCTION

Dimensionality reduction, including descending dimension algorithms, is another category of unsupervised learning. It transforms high-dimensional data into a lower number of dimensions through the compression of features, while still preserving as much variance in the data as possible. Dimensionality reduction does not necessarily delete data but rather merges a dataset's features (columns).

Consider, for example, a dataset with four columns containing the following features: room length, room width, Jacuzzi, and floor level. As the dataset has four features, it can be plotted on a four-dimensional (4-D) scatterplot.

However, we can remove redundant information and reduce the total number of dimensions to three by combining 'room length' and 'room width' and creating a new column titled 'room area.' Applying dimensionality reduction will thereby enable us to compress the scatterplot from 4-D to 3-D and conserve computational resources in the process. Another advantage of dimensionality reduction is visualization and ease of interpretation. Datasets with fewer dimensions are easier to interpret and share with a target audience.

Algorithms to perform dimensionality reduction include Principle Component Analysis (PCA) and *k*-means clustering. The latter performs data reduction by reducing the total number of data points by compressing rows in the table to a low number of clusters. If for example, *k* is set to 6, this will create 6 clusters. This will reduce the total number of rows (i.e. 60) to 6, each defined by the centroid location.

Principle Component Analysis, known also as General Factor Analysis, is an unsupervised approach used to examine interrelations among a set of variables.

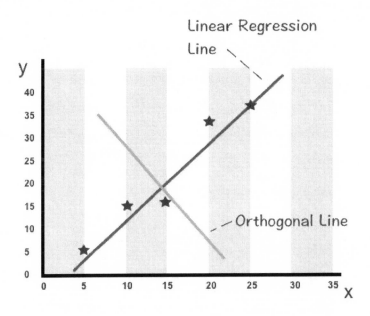

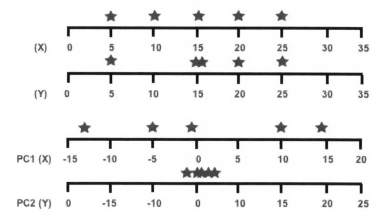

PCA relies on creating an orthogonal line perpendicular (at a right angle) to a regression hyperplane. The orthogonal line then takes the role of the y-axis.

Based on our new y-axis (created by the orthogonal line) the variance in values of PC2 has been minimized from the original x and y values. This can be seen from studying the four horizontal axes above, with the bottom two axes representing the new x and y values (PC1 & PC2).

We can now drop PC2 as it contributes the least to overall variance in our new scatterplot. This, in turn, allows us to focus our attention on studying the variance in PC1, which is greater.

PCA is particularly useful in reducing the dimensionality of three and four-dimensional scatterplots, especially as it is difficult to visually interpret data points in a high-dimensional space.

## 10

SUPPORT VECTOR MACHINE

As an advanced category of regression, support vector machine (SVM) resembles logistic regression but with stricter conditions. To that end, SVM is superior at drawing classification boundary lines. Let's examine what this looks like in action.

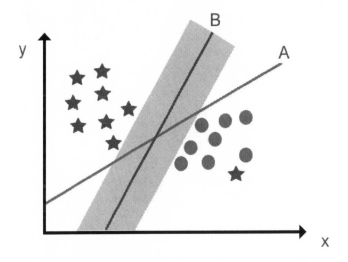

This scatterplot above contains data points that are linearly separable. The logistic hyperplane (A) splits the data points into two classes in a way that minimizes the distance between all data points and the hyperplane. The second line, hyperplane B (SVM), likewise separates the two clusters but from a position of maximum distance between itself and the two clusters.

You will also notice a gray area that denotes *margin*, which is the distance between the hyperplane and the nearest data point, multiplied by two. The margin is a key feature of SVM and is important because it offers additional support to cope with new data points that may infringe on a logistic regression hyperplane. To illustrate this potential scenario, let's consider the same scatterplot with the inclusion of a new data point.

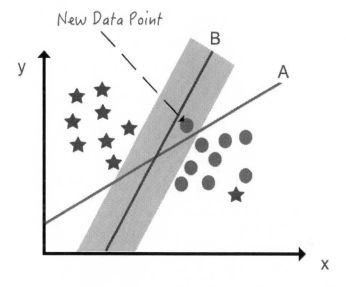

The new data point is a circle, but it is located incorrectly on the left side of the logistic regression hyperplane (designated for stars). The new data point, though, remains correctly located on the right side of the SVM hyperplane courtesy of ample 'support' supplied by the margin.

Another limitation of logistic regression is its sensitivity to anomalies (as seen in the scatterplot with the star in the bottom right corner). As visible in the example, hyperplane A (logistic regression) gravitates in the direction of the lone star. Conversely, SVM is less sensitive to anomalies and naturally minimizes their impact on overall classification through the location of its boundary line. SVM can thus be used as an effective method to mitigate the impact of anomalies.

The previous example comprised two features and was plotted on a two-dimensional plot. However, SVM's real strength can be found in high-dimensional data and with handling multiple features. SVM has numerous variations available to classify high-dimensional data, known as 'kernels,' including linear SVC, polynomial SVC, and the Kernel Trick. The Kernel Trick is an advanced solution to map data from a low-dimensional to a high-dimensional space. Transitioning from a two-dimensional to a three-dimensional space allows you to use a linear plane to split the data within a 3-D space as shown in the diagram.

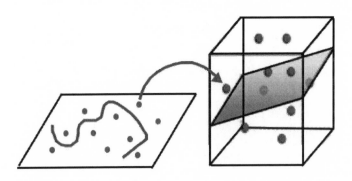

## 11

ARTIFICIAL NEURAL NETWORKS

We have so far examined a range of algorithms, but you might be wondering what grouping data points and drawing boundary lines has to do with machine learning and artificial intelligence?

We know that analyzing values from existing data is a way to predict the future. However, simple algorithms such as linear regression can be performed by hand—as seen in an earlier example—without troves of data and advanced computing power. While each of the algorithms seen so far falls into the camp of classical statistics, they become vital to machine learning when matched with larger datasets and advanced algorithms. It is now time to introduce deep learning.

Deep learning is a subfield of machine learning that analyzes data through layers and has become an immensely popular technique over the last five years following breakthroughs in GPU technology. Since 2012, scores of tech companies have gained attention for their work in deep layer analysis including Deepmind, which defeated the world champion, Lee Se-dol, in the game of Go in 2016, as well as other breakthroughs in image classification, machine translation, social network filtering, and speech recognition technology.

Deep learning is a new term for artificial neural networks (ANN), which has existed for well over fifty years—albeit prior to today's advanced technology. Four decades ago, neural networks were only two layers deep. In the past, it was computationally impossible to develop and analyze deep networks. Naturally, with the development of technology, it is now possible to analyze ten or more layers, or even over 100 layers of neurons. It's important to note, though, that very little has changed to algorithms over the last 40 years. The rapid gains have instead come from the size of the datasets and the computing power that we now have at our disposal to conduct sophisticated deep layer analysis. Powered by GPU technology on the cloud and converging with massive reserves of data, neural networks are used today by online companies such as Amazon to provide product recommendations and by Facebook to identify faces in photos.

The naming of artificial neural networks, also known as neural networks, was originally inspired by the human brain because of its resemblance to a set of interconnected brain cells or neurons. This analogy to the human brain often confuses students new to machine learning.

Two historical figures who were familiar with neuroscience were the men who coined this algorithm. With their sophisticated understanding of the human brain, Walter Pitts (1923-1969), a

Computational Neuroscientist and Warren McCulloch (1898-1969), a Neurophysiologist, observed a resemblance to the statistical approach of layered analysis. Similar to neurons in the human brain, neural networks are formed by interconnected neurons that interact with each other. Each connection has a numeric weight that can be altered based on experience. Much like building a human pyramid, neurons are stacked on top of each other and start with a broad base. The bottom layer consists of data such as text, images or sound, which are divided into what we call neurons. Each neuron then sends information to the next layer of neurons upon successful activation. If a threshold is not met, the next neuron is not activated.

This is also where shallow algorithms, such as linear regression, come into use. What makes deep learning 'deep' is the stacking of neurons containing shallow algorithms. Neurons are able to contain a range of shallow algorithms, including regression analysis, clustering, and decision trees. These algorithms are considered 'shallow' because unlike neural networks they do not analyze information through multiple layers.

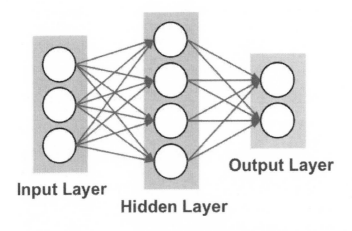

Output Layer

Input Layer

Hidden Layer

A simple neural network can be divided into input, hidden, and output layers. Data is first received by the input layer, where broad features are detected. The hidden layer(s) then analyze and process those data, and based on previous computations, the data becomes streamlined through the passing of each layer of neurons. The final result is shown as the output layer.

The middle layers are considered hidden layers because the data and calculations passing through these layers are not directly known. This is a similar concept to human sight. If you see four connected lines in the shape of a square you will immediately recognize those four lines as a square. You will not notice the lines as four independent objects with no relationship to each other. Our brain is conscious only to the final outcome of the recognition process and not the hidden layers.

Visually recognizing a square, however, is a step-by-step process. Each independent line (of which there are four) is processed by the first row of neurons. At the next layer of neurons, each independent line merges into two lines. At the third layer, the two lines merge into a single shape and via staged neuron processing our brain can visually recognize the square.

ANN works much the same way in that it breaks data down into layers, including hidden layers of analysis. The calculations made inside the hidden layers are not directly known because only neuron activation or activation failure is shown.

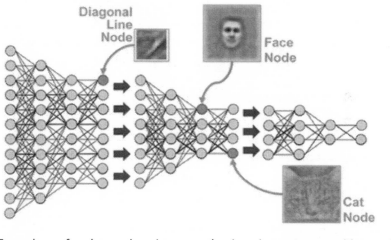

Example of deep learning used in image recognition. *Source: www.kdnuggets.com*

While there are many techniques to assemble the nodes of a neural network, the simplest method is the feed-forward network. In a feed-forward network, signals flow only in one direction and there is no loop in the network.

The most basic form of a feed-forward neural network is the *perceptron*.

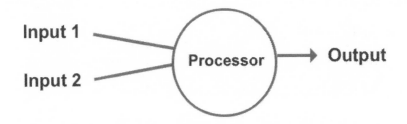

A perceptron consists of one or more inputs, a processor, and a single output. Within a perceptron model, inputs:

1) Are fed into the processor (neuron)

2) Are processed

3) Generate an output

As an example, say we have a perceptron made up of two inputs:

Input 1: $3x = 24$

Input 2: $2x = 16$

We then add a random weight to these two inputs and they are sent into the neuron to be processed.

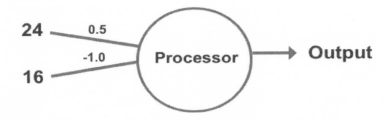

Weights

Input 1: 0.5

Input 2: -1.0

Next, we multiply each weight by its input:

Input 1: 24 * 0.5 = 12

Input 2: 16 * -1.0 = -16

Passing the sum of the edge weights through the activation function generates the perceptron's output.

A key feature of the perceptron is that it only registers two possible outcomes, '1' and '0'. A value of '1' triggers the activation function and a value of '0' does not. Although the perceptron is binary in nature (1 or 0), there are various ways in which we can configure the activation function. In this example, the activation function is ≥ 0. This means that if the sum is a positive number or zero, the output is 1. If the sum is a negative number, the output is 0.

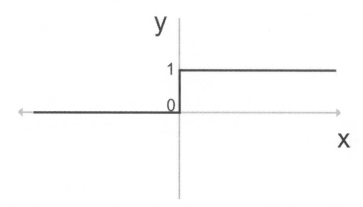

Thus:

Input 1: 24 * 0.5 = 12

Input 2: 16 * -1.0 = -16

Sum (Σ): 12 + -16 = - 4

As a numeric value less than zero, the result will register as '0' and therefore not trigger the activation function of the perceptron. However, we can modify the activation threshold to a completely different rule, such as:

$x > 3$, $y = 1$

$x \leq 3$, $y = 0$

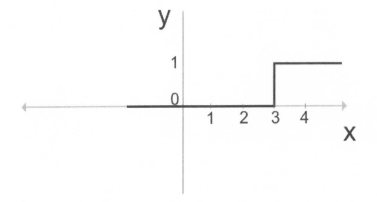

When working with a larger model of neural network layers, a value of '1' will be configured to pass the output to the next layer. Conversely, a '0' value is configured to be ignored and will not be passed to the next layer for processing.

The weakness of a perceptron is that, because the output is binary (0 or 1), small changes in the weights or bias in any single perceptron within a larger neural network can induce polarizing results. This can lead to dramatic changes within the network and a complete flip in the final output. As a result, this makes it very difficult to train an accurate model that can be successfully applied to test data and future data inputs.

An alternative to the perceptron is the *sigmoid neuron*. A sigmoid neuron is very similar to a perceptron, but the usage of the sigmoid function rather than a binary model now accepts any value between 0 and 1. This enables more flexibility to absorb small changes in edge weights without triggering inverse results—as the output is no longer binary. In other words, the output won't flip because of one minor change to an edge weight or input value.

$$y = \frac{1}{1+e^{-x}}$$

While more flexible than a perceptron, a sigmoid neuron cannot generate negative values. Hence, a third option is the *hyperbolic tangent function*.

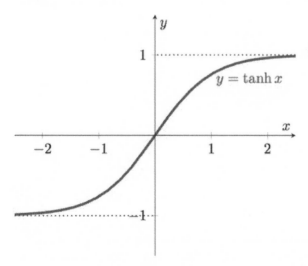

So far we have discussed basic neural networks. To create an advanced neural network, we link numerous perceptrons, sigmoid neurons or other basic neural models together in order to form a network with a deep number of layers. This is known as deep learning. There is no exact answer on how many layers should go into a deep learning network and Microsoft's vision recognition technology currently uses 152 layers!

## 12

BIAS & VARIANCE

Algorithm selection is an important step in forming an accurate model, but deploying that algorithm with a high-level of accuracy can be a challenging balancing act. The fact that each algorithm can produce vastly different models based on the hyperparameters provided can lead to dramatically different results. Hyperparameters are the algorithm's settings, similar to the controls on the dashboard of an airplane or the knobs used to tune the frequency on a radio.

A constant challenge in machine learning is navigating *underfitting* and *overfitting*, which describe how closely the model follows the actual patterns found in the dataset. To understand underfitting and overfitting, you first need to understand *bias* and *variance*.

Bias refers to the gap between your predicted value and the actual value. In the case of high bias, your errors are likely to be skewed in a certain direction and require modification. Variance describes how scattered your predicted values are. Bias and variance can be better understood by analyzing the following visual representation.

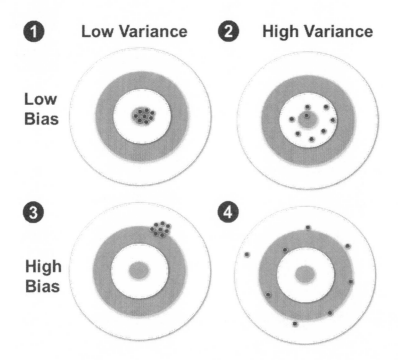

① Low Variance **②** High Variance

Low Bias

③

High Bias

④

Shooting targets, as shown here, are not a visual chart used in machine learning but can be used here to explain bias and variance. First, imagine that the center of the target, or the bull's-eye, perfectly predicts the correct value of your model. The dots marked on the target then represent an individual realization of your model based on the training data at hand.

In certain cases, the dots will be densely positioned close to the bull's-eye, ensuring that predictions made by the model are highly accurate. In other cases, the training data will contain outliers/anomalies and the hits will be scattered across the target. The more the dots deviate from the bull's-eye, the less accurate the model's predictions.

In the first target, we can see a case of low bias and low variance.

Bias is low because the hits are closely aligned to the center, and there is low variance because the hits are densely positioned in one location.

The second target shows a case of low bias and high variance. Although the hits are not as close to the bull's-eye as the previous example, they are still close to the center and bias is therefore relatively low. However, there is high variance because the hits are spread out from each other. The third target represents high bias and low variance, and the fourth target shows high bias and high variance.

Ideally, you want to reach a situation of low variance and low bias. In reality, however, there is more often a trade-off between optimal bias and variance. Bias and variance both contribute to error, but it is error that we wish to minimize, not bias or variance specifically, as seen in the following diagram.

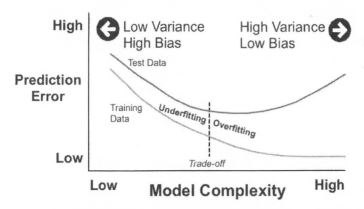

In this diagram we can see two lines. One line represents the test data and the other represents the training data. On the left, both lines start at a point of high prediction error due to low variance and high bias. As they move from left to right, they change to the opposite: high variance and low bias. This leads to low prediction error in the case of the training data but high error for the test data. In the middle of the chart is an optimal balance between prediction error, variance, and bias. This is a common case of bias-variance trade-off.

Mismanaging the bias-variance trade-off can lead to poor results from your model. As seen in the diagram, this can result in the model becoming overly simple and inflexible (underfitting) or overly complex and flexible (overfitting).

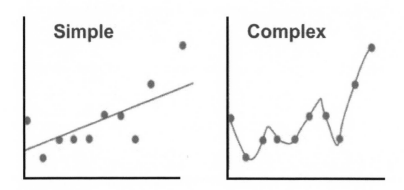

Underfitting (low variance, high bias) on the left and overfitting (high variance, low bias) on the right are clearly seen in these two scatterplots.

A natural temptation is to add complexity to the model (as shown on the right) until the model perfectly fits the training data. This leads to overfitting. The more your model bends itself to your exact training data, rather than the full dataset's underlying patterns, the more susceptible your model is to inaccurately predicting the test data. An overfitted model therefore yields accurate predictions from the training data and is less accurate at predicting from the test data. Alternatively, overfitting may be caused because your training and test data were not properly randomized.

Underfitting occurs when the model is overly simple, and again, has not scratched the surface of the dataset's underlying patterns. Underfitting can lead to inaccurate predictions for both the training and test data. Common causes of underfitting include insufficient training data to adequately cover all possible combinations, and situations where the training and test data were not properly randomized.

To eradicate both underfitting and overfitting, you may need to modify your model's hyperparameters to ensure that they best fit your training and test data. A suitable fit should acknowledge major trends in the data and play down or even omit minor variations. This may mean re-randomizing your training and test data or adding new data points in order to better detect underlying patterns. However, in most instances, you will need to consider switching algorithms or modifying your hyperparameters based on trial and error in order to minimize the issue of the bias-variance trade-off.

Specifically, this might entail switching from linear regression to multi-linear regression to reduce bias by increasing variance. Or it might mean increasing 'k' in k-NN to reduce variance (by averaging together more neighbors). A third example could be reducing variance by switching from a single decision tree (which is prone to overfitting) to a random forest with multiple decision trees.

Another effective strategy to combat overfitting and underfitting is to introduce *regularization*. Regularization artificially amplifies bias error by penalizing an increase in a model's complexity. In effect, this add-on parameter provides a warning alert to keep high variance in check while the original parameters are being optimized.

## 13

DECISION TREES

The fact that neural networks can be used to solve far more machine learning challenges than any other technique has led some pundits to hail neural networks as the ultimate machine learning algorithm. However, this is not to say that neural networks fit the bill as a statistical silver bullet. In numerous cases, neural networks fall short and decision trees are held up as a popular counterargument.

The massive reserve of data and computational resources that neural networks demand is one downside. Only after training on millions of tagged examples can Google's image recognition engine reliably recognize classes of simple objects (such as dogs). But how many dogs do you need to show to the average five-year-old before they 'get it?'

Decision trees, on the other hand, provide a high-level of efficiency as well as easy interpretation. These two benefits make this simple algorithm highly effective in the space of machine learning.

As a supervised learning technique, decision trees are used primarily for solving classification problems, but they can be applied to solve regression problems too.

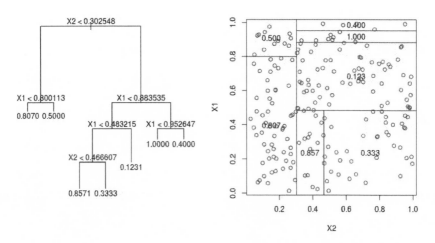

Example of a regression tree. Source: http://freakonometrics.hypotheses.org/

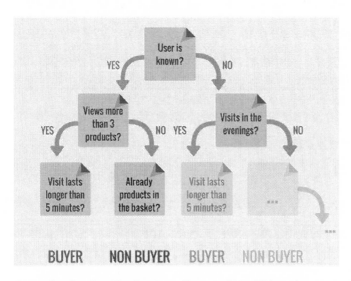

Example of a classification tree. Source: http://blog.akanoo.com

Classification trees use quantitative and categorical data to model categorical outcomes. Regression trees also use quantitative and categorical data but instead model quantitative outcomes.

Decision trees themselves start with a root node, which acts as a starting point (at the top) and is followed by splits that produce branches. The statistical/mathematical term for these branches is *edges*. The branches then link to leaves, known also as nodes, which form decision points. A final leaf that does not generate any new branches constitutes a terminal node, which provides the final output.

Decision trees thus not only break down and explain how classification or regression is formulated, but they also produce a neat visual flowchart you can show to others. The ease of interpretation is a strong advantage of decision trees as well as their ability to make sense of both high dimensional and large quantities of data. Decision trees can also be applied to a wide range of use cases.

Real-life examples include image recognition, picking a scholarship recipient, assessing an applicant for a home loan, predicting e-commerce sales or selecting the right job applicant. When a customer or applicant queries why they weren't selected for a particular scholarship, home loan, job, etc., you can pass the decision tree over and let them see the decision-making process with their own eyes.

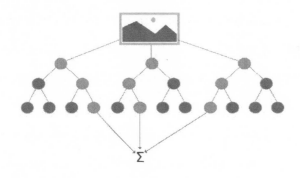

Example of a decision tree used in image recognition

How to Create a Decision Tree?

Decision trees are built by first splitting data into two groups. This binary splitting process is then repeated at each branch (layer). The aim is to select a binary question that best splits the data into two homogenous groups at each branch of the tree, such that it minimizes the level of data entropy at the next.

Entropy is a mathematical term that explains the measure of variance in the data amongst different classes. In simple terms, we want the data at each layer to be more homogenous than at the last.

We thus want to pick a 'greedy' algorithm that can reduce the level of entropy at each layer of the tree. One such greedy algorithm is the Iterative Dichotomizer (ID3), invented by J.R. Quinlan. This is one of three decision tree implementations developed by Quinlan, hence the '3'.

ID3 applies entropy to determine which binary question to ask at each layer of the decision tree. At each layer, ID3 identifies a variable (converted into a binary question) that will produce the least entropy at the next layer.

Let's have a look at the following example to better understand how this works.

Employees	Exceeded KPIs	Leadership Capability	Aged < 30	Outcome
6	6	2	3	Promoted
4	0	2	4	Not promoted

Variable 1 produces:

- Six promoted employees who exceeded their Key Performance Indicators (Yes)

- Four employees who didn't exceed their KPIs and were not promoted (No)

Variable 1 produces two homogenous groups at the next layer of the decision tree.

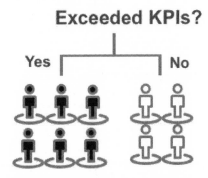

Black = Promoted, White = Not Promoted

Variable 2 produces:

- Two promoted employees with leadership capabilities (Yes)

- Four promoted employees with **no** leadership capabilities (No)

- Two employees with leadership capabilities who were not promoted (Yes)

- Two employees with **no** leadership capabilities who were not promoted (No)

Variable 2 produces two groups of mixed data points.

Black = Promoted, White = Not Promoted

Variable 3 produces:

- Three promoted employees aged under thirty (Yes)

- Three promoted employees aged over thirty (No)

- Four employees aged under thirty who were not promoted (Yes)

Variable 3 produces one homogenous group and one mixed group of data points.

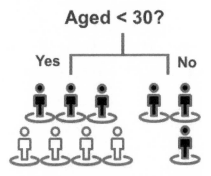

Black = Promoted, White = Not Promoted

Of these three variables, variable 1 produces the best result with two perfectly homogenous groups. Variable 3 produces the second best result, as one leaf is homogenous. Variable 2 produces two leaves that are not homogenous. Variable 1 would thus be selected as the first binary question to split this dataset.

Whether it is ID3 or another algorithm, the process of splitting data into binary partitions, known as *recursive partitioning*, is repeated until a *stopping criterion* is met. This stopping point can be based on various criteria, such as:

- When all leaves contain less than 3-5 items
- When a branch produces a result that places all items into one binary leaf

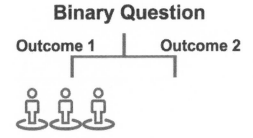

Example of a stopping criteria

A caveat to remember when using decision trees is their susceptibility to overfitting. The cause of overfitting, in this case, is the training data. Taking into account the classification rules that exist in the training data, a decision tree is precise at training the first round of data. However, that decision tree model produced by the training data may not apply to the test data due to the existence of new patterns. In this case, either the training data and/or test data are not representative of the entire dataset. Moreover, because decision trees are formed from repeatedly splitting data points into two partitions, a slight change in how the data is split at the top or middle of the tree can dramatically alter the final results. This can produce a different tree altogether! The offender, in this case, is our greedy algorithm.

From the very first split of the data, the greedy algorithm selects binary questions that best partition data into two homogenous groups. But, like a young boy sitting in front of a box of cupcakes, the greedy algorithm is oblivious to the future repercussions of its short-term actions. The binary question it applies to initially split the data does not guarantee accuracy in regards to the final outcome. Rather, a less efficient initial split may produce a more accurate outcome.

In sum, decision trees are highly visual and effective at classifying a single set of data. However, decision trees can be inflexible and vulnerable to overfitting.

Random Forests

Rather than striving for the most efficient split at each round of recursive partitioning, an alternative technique is to construct multiple trees and combine their predictions to select an optimal path of classification. This involves a randomized selection of binary questions to grow multiple different decision trees, known as *random forests*.

The process of combining statistical techniques to create a unified model is known as ensemble modeling. Ensemble models can be generated using a single technique with numerous variations, known as a homogeneous ensemble, or through different techniques, known as a heterogeneous ensemble. Random forests are an example of homogeneous ensemble modeling.

The key to understanding random forests is to understand bootstrap sampling. As you can guess, there's little use in building five or ten identical models—there needs to be some variation. That's why bootstrap sampling draws on the same dataset but extracts a different variation of the data at each turn as a form of statistical resampling. The full training dataset is available at each turn, also known as 'with replacement.'

In growing random forests, multiple variations of the training data are run through each of the trees. The results from each tree are compared and voted on to create an optimal tree to produce the final model or what is known as the 'final class.'

The 'random' component of 'random forests' is due to the

randomness of both the data selected for each tree and the binary questions that dictate how each tree is split. Each decision tree therefore uses a slightly different set of data and while this does not eliminate the existence of anomalies, it does aid in mitigating their impact. Naturally, the dominant patterns in the dataset will appear in a higher number of trees and this will emerge in the final class.

Secondly, the randomness of the binary questions selected has a dramatic impact on the overall tree. Unlike a decision tree which has a full set of features/ variables to choose from, random forests have a limited number of features/variables available to build binary decisions. If all trees inspected a full set of features, they would inevitably look the same, because they would each seek to maximize information gain at the subsequent layer and thereby select the optimal feature at each split. However, due to the limited number of features shown and the randomized data it is given, random forests do not generate a single highly optimized tree comparable to a lone decision tree. Rather, random forests embrace randomness and through sheer volume are capable of providing a reliable result with potentially less variance and overfitting than a single decision tree.

In general, random forests favor a high number of trees (i.e. 100+) to smooth out the potential impact of anomalies, but there is, though, a diminishing rate of effectiveness as more new trees are added. At a certain level, new trees may not add any significant improvement to your model, but they will definitely extend your processing time!

While it will depend on your exact dataset, 100-150 decision trees is often a recommended starting point. Author and data expert, Scott Hartshorn, advises that you first focus on optimizing other hyperparameters before adding more trees to the initial model, as this will reduce your processing time in the short-term and you know that increasing the number of trees later should provide at least some benefit.[4]

A drawback, however, of using random forests is that you do sacrifice the visual simplicity and ease of interpretation that comes with a single decision tree, instead returning to a black-box technique.

Gradient Boosting

Another homogenous ensemble learning model similar to random forests is the popular technique of *gradient boosting.* Rather than selecting combinations of binary questions at random, gradient boosting selects binary questions that will improve prediction accuracy for each new tree. Decision trees are therefore grown sequentially, as each tree is created using information derived from the previous decision tree.

---

[4] Scott Hartshorn, *Machine Learning With Random Forests And Decision Trees: A Visual Guide For Beginners*, 2016

The way this works is that mistakes incurred with the training data are recorded and then applied to the next round of training data. For each iteration, weights are added to the training data based on the results of the previous iteration. Higher weighting is applied to instances that were incorrectly predicted and instances that were correctly predicted receive less weighting. The training and test data are then compared and errors are again logged in order to inform weighting at each subsequent round. Earlier iterations that do not perform well, and that perhaps misclassified data, can thus be improved upon through further iterations.

This process is repeated until there is a low rate of error. The final result is then obtained from a weighted average of the total predictions derived from each model. While this approach mitigates the issue of overfitting, it does so with fewer trees than the bagging approach. In general, the more trees you add to a random forest, the greater its ability to counter overfitting. Conversely, with gradient boosting too many trees can cause overfitting and caution must be taken as new trees are added.

## 14

ASSOCIATION ANALYSIS

Association analysis and recommender systems are our next two algorithm categories. Both algorithm categories apply to analyzing data and identifying items that are commonly associated together; such as frequent purchase combinations, movie combinations, or linking users on a social media network that have shared attributes. Through identifying relevant and common combinations, companies can strategically showcase and recommend items to customers and increase their key performance metrics, including sales, traffic growth or user engagement.

While association analysis and recommender systems resemble each other in their goal to improve conversion through analyzing popular combinations, they are far from the same. They differ both in regards to input data and in their unit of aggregation (time).

The unit of aggregation for association analysis is the current session. A current session could be the video clip you are currently watching on YouTube or this week's visit to your local Walmart store. Your previous sessions, however, are not included as input data. In association analysis, the algorithm has no knowledge of what videos you previously watched on YouTube or what you bought at Walmart last week. Association analysis focuses solely on the current session and is impervious to the historical data of the individual user.

Whereas association analysis integrates no knowledge about the user's previous sessions, recommender systems absorb and aggregate the user's previous sessions directly into its model. This allows for a much more personalized approach to recommending items. We will examine recommender systems in the next chapter, but for now we will focus our attention on association analysis.

The ultimate aim of association analysis is to maximize the number of products that go into a customer's basket. This explains why association analysis has earned the moniker of *market basket analysis*.

An example of association analysis could be an e-commerce store customizing promotions on their checkout page. When a customer purchases BBQ tongs, they are subsequently offered a discounted price on a bag of charcoal. The e-commerce website has no information to draw on regarding the customer's previous purchasing behavior, including whether the customer has previously purchased charcoal. Nor does the e-commerce site know whether the customer's BBQ is electric or charcoal-fuelled, or whether the customer even has a BBQ! As a generic recommendation mechanism, the sole focus of association analysis is on identifying relationships between items in the dataset.

Association analysis is most effective in offline retail, as there is typically no on-record information regarding customers' previous purchase sessions. Retailers conduct association analysis on items that are commonly purchased together and utilize this information to dictate store layout and what products are showcased together. For example, research has shown that flashlights and essential supplies such as bottles of water are an effective product combination in the lead-up to a storm.

The first step in conducting association analysis is to construct a **frequent itemset** (X). Frequent itemsets are a combination of items that regularly appear together, or have an affinity for each other. The combination could be one item with another single item.

To create a frequent itemset, we first have to calculate support (SUPP). Support calculates how common an individual item or set of items appear within the dataset. Support can be calculated by dividing X by T, where X is how often an individual item appears in the dataset and T is your total number of transactions. For example, if bread buns only feature in 6 of a total of 10 transactions, then the support for that item will be 6/10 = 0.6. If sausages appear in 8 of 10 transactions, the support for sausages is 8/10 = 0.8.

An itemset can also contain multiple items, such as 'hamburger buns and onions.' In this case, the support would be calculated using the same formula of X over T. In other words, how often do hamburger buns and onions appear together in the same transaction.

In order to save time and focus on items with higher support, you need to set a minimum level known as **minimal support** or **minsup**. Applying minsup will allow you to ignore low-level cases of support. For example, you may choose to ignore itemsets with support of less than 0.1. A frequent itemset is generated when an itemset, such as bread buns and onions, passes the minimum support of 0.1.

The final step in association analysis is **rule generation**. Rule generation is a collection of if/then statements, in which you calculate what is known as confidence. Confidence is a metric similar to conditional probability.

This is expressed as (A => B)

A is the first item purchased or consumed. B is the subsequent item purchased or consumed given that A has also been purchased/consumed.

Following with our supermarket analogy, let's say 'A' is 'bread,' and 'B' is 'sausages.'

Bread => Sausages

This means that if bread is purchased, what is the subsequent likelihood of sausages being purchased in the same transaction?

Alternatively, the combination could be two or more items with one or more other items, i.e. bread + onions => Sausages. Which means what is the likelihood of sausages being purchased given that bread and onions are already in the customer's basket?

The calculation of confidence is expressed as follows: Supp(X U Y) / Supp(X)

Where U = union. In this example, let's say that bread and sausages appear in 4/10 transactions. Their combined support (union) is 0.4.

0.4/0.6 = 0.66

The confidence of sausages appearing in the same transaction as bread is thus 0.66, or 66%.

Similar to minimal support, we can also set a minimum level of confidence known as **minimal confidence**, which will enable us to ignore low-level cases. If the association rule of bread => sausages passes minimum confidence, it is known as a strong association rule.

Numerous machine learning models can be applied to conduct association analysis. Below is a list of the most common algorithms:

- Apriori

- Eclat (equivalence class transformations)

- FP-growth (frequent pattern)

- RElim (recursive elimination)

- SaM (split and merge)

- JIM (Jaccard itemset mining)

The most common association analysis algorithm model is Apriori. Apriori is applied to calculate support for itemsets one item at a time. It finds the support of one item (how common is that item in the dataset) and determines whether there is support for that item. If the support happens to be less than the designated minimum support amount (minsup) that you have set, the item will be ignored. Apriori will then move on to the next item and evaluate the minsup value and determine whether it should hold on to the item or ignore it and move on.

After the algorithm has completed all single-item evaluations, it will transition to processing two-item itemsets. The same minsup criteria is applied to gather items that meet the minsup value. As you can probably guess, it then proceeds to analyze three-item combinations and so on.

The downside of the Apriori method is that the processing time can be slow; it is demanding on computational resources, and the demand on time and resources grows exponentially at each round of analysis. This approach can therefore be inefficient at processing large datasets.

A popular alternative is Eclat. Eclat again calculates support for a single itemset, but should the minsup value be successfully reached, it proceeds directly to adding an additional item (now a two-item itemset). This is different to Apriori, which would move to processing the next single item and first processing all single items. Eclat, on the other hand, will seek to add as many items to the original single item as possible, until it fails to reach the set minsup.

This approach is faster and less intensive in regards to computational resources and memory, but the itemsets produced are normally long and difficult to manipulate.

## 15

RECOMMENDER SYSTEMS

Recommender systems differ from association analysis in that they provide personalized combinations. They focus on the aggregate behavior and historical relationship between the user/consumer and the items available.

It's important to note that recommender systems are not a specific algorithm but rather a practical application of machine learning (like association analysis) that incorporate various popular machine learning algorithms including logistic regression and principle component analysis. The two most common recommender system approaches are content-based filtering and collaborative filtering.

Content-based Filtering

Content-based filtering recommends items to a user based on similar items correlated with purchasing behavior. Content-based filtering relies on both a description of the item (meta data) and profiling of user preferences. Under this model, products must be adequately described in the form of keywords/meta data, and likewise, user preferences need to be known and recorded.

User preferences can be determined by examining past purchasing/consumption behavior, web browsing history, and documented personal details such as gender, location, nationality, and hobbies or interests. From information gleaned about the user, content-based filtering can be applied to compare that data with the description of items available and predict items to suggest to the user.

As long as items are properly tagged and there is sufficient data regarding the individual user and their previous behavior, content-based filtering can be a highly effective approach.

The downside of content-based filtering is that while recommendations are generally accurate, they are limited in variety and rely heavily on specific item and user descriptions. For platforms with massive amounts of items, this can involve considerable upfront effort to catalogue new items.

Collaborative Filtering

Collaborative filtering recommends items to a user based on predictions formed by collecting and analyzing other users' historical purchasing or consumption habits. A common way of expressing this is *people who buy x also buy y*. Indicators of user interest include product ratings, likes, traffic, purchases, conversions, time-on-page, and viewing habits (e.g. watching a video or film to the end).

Collaborative filtering can be seen all over the Internet and Amazon's own product recommender system is a popular example. Social media sites such as Facebook, Twitter and LinkedIn also utilize collaborative filtering to recommend groups and social connections to users based on similar group memberships and the social connections of other users in a given network.

Collaborative filtering recommenders are typically designed to generate results from users with shared interests. For instance, the online music platform Soundify knows that fans of hard metal music who enjoy listening to Song A also enjoy listening to Song B. Soundify can also determine if a given user fits the category of heavy metal enthusiast based on their previous listening habits. Soundify will thus recommend heavy metal enthusiasts to listen to Song B after listening to Song A based on similar user preferences.

A primary advantage of collaborative filtering is that because it analyzes user behavior, it doesn't need to rely on a complex understanding of the actual item and the specific attributes of the item it is recommending. It is also more flexible at reacting to changes in user/consumer behavior, but it can be susceptible to sudden changes in fashion, pop culture, and lifestyle design.

A challenge and potential downside to collaborative filtering is the large amount of upfront data that is required. Additionally, the scalability of such systems can become computationally challenging for platforms with millions of users. Lastly, collaborative filtering is highly vulnerable to people doing the wrong thing and gaming the system. This includes driving artificial traffic to product items, creating fake users, or fabricating a system of actions to cheat the system, also known as a shilling attack.

One technique to minimize this issue is to limit analysis to user purchases, rather than browsing habits, as the former is harder to fabricate. That said, fake online purchases remain rampant and malicious groups are becoming more elaborate in their tactics to game recommender systems. Mitigating the influence of shilling attacks in machine learning is a hot topic and a potentially lucrative area of study to consider.

The Hybrid Approach

An alternative to relying solely on collaborative and content-based filtering is what is known as the hybrid approach. This third approach draws on both collaborative and content-based filtering techniques to generate recommendations to users. The flexibility of this approach helps to soften the edges and potential downsides of content-based and collaborative filtering techniques.

In practice, a hybrid approach recommender can be implemented by separating content-based and collaborative filtering and combining their predictions, or by creating a unified and integrated approach. Many popular online platforms including Netflix utilize a hybrid approach.

## 16

ALGORITHM SELECTION

By now you are familiar with the basics of various core machine learning algorithms. But how do you know when to use which algorithm?

Firstly, there are certain algorithms that are obvious for solving specific problems, such as dimension reduction. But not all situations are this clear-cut.

Secondly, a neural network, as we have covered, is generally regarded as the most versatile machine learning technique because it can be used to solve a broad spectrum of machine learning problems. However, as we know, the reality is more nuanced. As neural networks tend to be the most data and time intensive of machine learning algorithms, simpler algorithms such as decision trees and k-nearest neighbors are often a better choice. The computing resources you have available and/or time limitations can be a primary consideration in selecting the right algorithm.

In addition, the size of the training dataset will also impact your decision. Neural networks require significant amounts of data to run effectively and are more cost-effective and time-efficient when working with large quantities of data.

Next, you will need to diagnose whether your dataset requires a supervised or unsupervised approach. If the data are labeled, this will narrow your selection down to a narrower range of supervised learning algorithms. If the data are not labeled, then you are likely to opt for an unsupervised algorithm.

Lastly, there is the option of testing multiple algorithms and evaluating their accuracy and results on the dataset at hand. This entails pushing a number of algorithms through your training and test data and assessing the prediction accuracy of each algorithm to find the best fit.

The following table shows the results of various machine learning techniques, and their accuracy in diagnosing heart disease based on academic studies conducted using the Cleveland Heart Disease Dataset.

Cleveland Heart Disease Dataset

Author/Year	Technique	Accuracy
(Cheung 2001)	Decision Tree	81.11%
	Naïve Bayes	81.48%
(Polat , Sahan et al. 2007)	k-nearest Neighbor	87.00%
(Tu, Shin et al. 2009)	Bagging Algorithm	81.41%
(Das, Turkoglu et al. 2009)	Neural Network	89.01%
(Shouman, et al 2011)	Nine Voting Equal Frequency Discretization Gain Ratio Decision Tree	84.10%

Source: International Journal of Information and Education Technology, Vol. 2, No.

3, June 2012

The table illustrates two patterns we already know. First, neural networks prove to be a clear leader in regards to accuracy (89.01%). Second, alternative algorithms can be applied with slightly inferior accuracy but with benefits in other areas. The *k*-NN algorithm, in this case, produces an accuracy rate of 87 percent, despite its comparative simplicity. While *k*-NN does demand larger memory requirements to store sample data than other algorithms, it is a cost-effective and easy to implement alternative to a neural network.

If you wish to learn more about algorithm selection, you can view this decision tree from Scikit-learn:

http://scikit-learn.org/stable/tutorial/machine_learning_map/

## 17

BUILDING A MODEL IN PYTHON

After examining the statistical underpinnings of various algorithms, it's now time to turn our attention to building an actual machine learning model. Although there are numerous options in regards to programming languages (as outlined in Chapter 4), for this exercise we will use Python because it is quick to learn and it's an effective programming language for anyone interested in manipulating and working with large datasets.

If you don't have any experience in programming or programming with Python, there's no need to worry. The key purpose of this chapter is to understand the methodology and steps behind building a basic machine learning model and not memorizing specific code.

In this exercise, we will design a system to predict the global sales of video games using gradient boosting by performing the following six steps:

1) Set up the development environment

2) Import the dataset

3) Scrub the dataset

4) Split the data into training and test data

5) Select an algorithm and configure its hyperparameters

6) Evaluate the results

1) Set up the development environment

The first step is to prepare our development environment. For this exercise, we will be working in Jupyter Notebook, which is an open-source web application that allows editing and sharing of notebooks.

You can download Jupyter Notebook from: http://jupyter.org/install.html

Jupyter Notebook can be installed using the Anaconda Distribution or Python's package manager, pip. There are instructions available on the Jupyter Notebook website that outline both options. As an experienced Python user, you may wish to install Jupyter Notebook via pip. For beginners, I recommend selecting the Anaconda Distribution option, which offers an easy click-and-drag setup. This particular installation option will direct you to the Anaconda website. From there, you can select your preferred installation for Windows, macOS, or Linux. Again, you can find instructions available on the Anaconda website according to your choice of operating system.

After installing Anaconda to your machine, you will have access to a number of data science applications including rstudio, Jupyter Notebook, and graphviz for data visualization. For this exercise, you will need to select Jupyter Notebook by clicking on 'Launch' in the Jupyter Notebook tab.

To initiate Jupyter Notebook, run the following command from the Terminal (for Mac/Linux) or Command Prompt (for Windows):

```
jupyter notebook
```

Terminal/Command Prompt will then generate a URL for you to copy and paste into your web browser. Example: http://localhost:8888/
Copy and paste the generated URL into your web browser to load Jupyter Notebook.

Once you have Jupyter Notebook open in your browser, click on 'New' in the top right-hand corner of the web application to create a new 'Notepad' project and then select 'Python 3'.

The final step is to install the necessary libraries required to complete this exercise. You will need to install Pandas and a number of libraries from Scikit-learn into the notepad.

In machine learning, each project will vary in regards to the libraries required for import. For this particular exercise, we are using gradient boosting (a type of ensemble modeling) and mean absolute error to measure performance.

You will need to import each of the following libraries and functions by entering these exact commands in Jupyter Notebook:

```
import pandas as pd
from sklearn.model_selection import train_test_split
from sklearn import ensemble
from sklearn.metrics import mean_absolute_error
from sklearn.externals import joblib
```

Don't worry if you don't recognize each of the imported libraries in the code snippet above. These libraries will be referred to in later steps.

2) Import the dataset

The next step is to import the dataset. For this exercise, I have selected a free and publicly available dataset from kaggle.com, which contains popular video game with sales greater than 100,000 copies. The dataset contains 17,416 video games and 15 variables including Name, Platform, Year, Genre, Publisher, NA Sales (North America), EU Sales (Europe), JP Sales (Japan), Other Sales (other regions), Global Sale, etc.

You can locate and download the dataset from this link: https://www.kaggle.com/kendallgillies/video-game-sales-and-ratings

After registering a free account and logging into kaggle.com, download the dataset as a zip file. Next, unzip the downloaded file and import into Jupyter Notebook.

To import the dataset, you can use the read_csv function to load the data into a Pandas dataframe.

```
df = pd.read_csv('~/Downloads/Video_Game_Sales_as_of_Jan_2017.csv')
```

This command will directly import the dataset into your notebook. However, take note that the exact path will depend on the saved location of the dataset on your machine.

3) Scrub the dataset

The next step is to scrub the dataset. Remember, scrubbing is the process of refining your dataset. This involves modifying or removing incomplete, irrelevant or duplicated data. It may also entail converting text-based data to numerical values and the redesigning of features.

Let's first remove columns from our dataset that we don't wish to include in the model by using the del df[' '] function and entering the vector (column) titles that we wish to remove. Please note that comments in the code are signaled with a hash (#) and are not processed by the machine, but they are useful for personal reference.

```
# Delete columns that we wish to remove
del df['Name']
del df['EU_Sales ']
del df['JP_Sales ']
del df['Other_Sales ']
```

The Name of the video game is not included in the model because each video game name is discrete (which means every game has a different name) and gradient boosting is not adequate to analyze patterns between a game's name and its relationship to financial success (measured in sales). Natural language processing (NLP) and text mining would be more suitable in this case to identify keywords or alliteration that impact the popularity of the game.

We've also left out EU Sales, Japan Sales, and Other Sales from our model because the aim is to predict Global Sales after releasing the game in the North America market. If Global Sales are predicted to be higher than USD $1 million after an initial release in the United States, we can then raise further capital to launch our game in overseas markets such as Europe and Japan—this is all hypothetical of course!

The remaining 10 independent variables in the dataset are Platform, Year of Release, Genre, Publisher, NA Sales (North America Sales), Critic Score, Critic Count, User Score, User Count, and Rating. The 15th variable, located in the tenth column of the dataset, is the dependent variable, which is Global Sales. Please note that sales figures in this dataset are represented in millions. Therefore a value of 1.0 is equivalent to USD $1 million.

The next step is to remove any missing values. Although there are numerous methods to populate missing values (i.e. calculating the mean, the median, or deleting missing values altogether), for this exercise, we want to keep it as simple as possible and we will therefore not be examining rows with missing values. The obvious drawback is that we have less data to analyze. As a beginner, it makes sense to master complete datasets before adding an extra dimension of difficulty in attempting to deal with missing values.

The following Pandas function can be used to remove rows with missing values.

```
df.dropna(axis=0, how='any', thresh=None, subset=None,
inplace=True)
```

Keep in mind that it's important to drop rows with missing values after applying the del df function (as shown in the previous step). This way, there's a better chance that more rows from the original dataset will be preserved.

Next, let's convert columns containing non-numerical data to numerical values by using one-hot encoding. One-hot encoding is a method to convert categorical data features into a binary format, represented as '1' or '0.' These two numbers represent 'True' or 'False'. A '0' represents False, the feature does not belong to a particular category. Whereas '1' is True, or hot, and denotes that the feature does belong to a particular category.

With Pandas, one-hot encoding can be performed using the get_dummies function:

```
features_df = pd.get_dummies(df, columns=['Platform',
'Publisher', 'Genre', 'Rating'])
```

This command converts column values for Platform, Publisher, Genre, and Rating into numerical values through the application of one-hot encoding.

Next, we need to remove the 'Global Sales' column because this column will act as our y (dependent) variable and for now we are only examining the ten X (independent) variables.

```
del features_df['Global_Sales']
```

Finally, create X and y arrays from the dataset using the matrix data type (as_matrix). The X array contains the independent variables and the y array contains the dependent variable of Global Sales.

```
X = features_df.as_matrix()
y = df['Global_Sales'].as_matrix()
```

4) Split the dataset

We are now at the stage of splitting the data into training and test segments. For this exercise, we will proceed with a standard 70/30 split by calling the Scikit-learn function below with an argument of '0.3'. The dataset's rows are also shuffled randomly to avoid bias using the random_state function.

```
X_train, X_test, y_train, y_test = train_test_split(X,
y, test_size=0.3, random_state=0)
```

5) Select the algorithm and configure its hyperparameters

As you will recall, we are using the gradient boosting algorithm for this exercise, as demonstrated below.

```
model = ensemble.GradientBoostingRegressor(
    n_estimators=150,
    learning_rate=0.1,
    max_depth=4,
    min_samples_split=4,
    min_samples_leaf=4,
    max_features=0.5,
    loss='huber'
)
```

The first line is the algorithm itself (gradient boosting) and comprises just one line of code. The lines below dictate the hyperparameters for this algorithm.

n_estimators represents how many decision trees to build. Remember that a high number of trees will generally improve accuracy (up to a certain point), but they will also increase the model's processing time. Above, I have selected 150 decision trees as an initial starting point.

learning_rate controls the rate at which additional decision trees influence the overall prediction. This effectively shrinks the contribution of each tree by the set learning_rate. Inserting a low rate here, such as 0.1, should improve accuracy.

max_depth defines the maximum number of layers (depth) for each decision tree. If 'None' is selected, then nodes expand until all leaves are pure or until all leaves contain less than min_samples_leaf.

min_samples_split defines the minimum number of samples required to implement a new binary split. For example, min_samples_split = 10 means there must be 10 available samples in order to create a new branch.

min_samples_leaf represents the minimum number of samples that must appear in each child node (leaf) before a new branch can be created. This helps to mitigate the impact of outliers and anomalies in the form of a low number of samples found in one leaf as a result of a binary split. For example, min_samples_leaf = 4 requires there to be at least four available samples within each leaf in order for a new branch to be created.

max_features is the total number of features presented to the model when determining the best split. As mentioned in Chapter 13, random forests and gradient boosting restrict the total number of features shown to each individual tree in order to create multiple classifiers that can be voted upon later.

If the max_features value is an integer (whole number), the model will consider max_features at each split (branch). If the value is a float (e.g. 0.6), then max_features is the percentage of total features randomly selected. Although max_features sets a maximum number of features to consider in identifying the best split, total features may exceed the max_features limit if no split is initially found.

loss calculates the model's error rate. For this exercise, we are using huber which protects against outliers and anomalies. Alternative error rate options include ls (least squares regression), lad (least absolute deviations), and quantile (quantile regression). Huber is actually a combination of ls and lad.

To learn more about gradient boosting hyperparameters, you may refer to the Scikit-learn website:

http://scikit-learn.org/stable/modules/generated/sklearn.ensemble.Gradient BoostingRegressor.html

After imputing the model's hyperparameters, we will implement Scikit-learn's fit function to start the model training process.

```
model.fit(X_train, y_train)
```

Lastly, we need to use Scikit-learn again to save the training model as a file using the joblib.dump function, which was imported into Jupyter Notebook in Step 1. Why do we need to save the code as a file? Because it will allow us to use the training model again in the future for predicting new values, without needing to rebuild the model from scratch.

```
joblib.dump(model, 'videogames_trained_model.pkl')
```

6) Evaluate the results

As mentioned earlier, for this exercise we will apply mean absolute error to evaluate the accuracy of the model.

```
mse = mean_absolute_error(y_train, model.predict(X_train))
print ("Training Set Mean Absolute Error: %.4f" % mse)
```

Here, we input our y values, which represent the correct results from the training dataset. The model.predict function is then called on the X training set and generates a prediction. The mean absolute error function will then compare the difference between the model's expected predictions and the actual values. The same process is repeated with the test dataset.

```
mse = mean_absolute_error(y_test, model.predict(X_test))
print ("Test Set Mean Absolute Error: %.4f" % mse)
```

Let's now run the entire program by right-clicking and pressing 'Run' or navigating from the Jupyter Notebook menu: Cell > Run All

Wait a few seconds for the computer to process the training model. The results, as shown below, will then appear at the bottom of the notepad.

```
Training Set Mean Absolute Error: 0.1512
Test Set Mean Absolute Error: 0.1982
```

For this exercise, our training set mean absolute error is 0.1512 or $151,200 and the test set mean absolute error is 0.1982 or $198,200. This means that on average, the model miscalculated actual Global Sales for each video game by $151,200 using the training data, and miscalculated by an average of $198,200 using the test data. This means that our model is relatively accurate at predicting the actual value of global sales using the training and test data.

However, we should keep in mind that approximately 78% of video games in the dataset accumulated less than $1 million in Global Sales. Thus, to miscalculate by $151,200-$198,200 does represent a reasonable rate of error that could lead to potentially poor commercial decisions for our hypothetical game company—especially if our game is not set to become a best seller!

The model does not have a high gap between the training and test data predictions. This gives us confidence that the model will produce a consistent margin of error when predicting future data not contained in the original model.

The fact that the training data is more accurate on average than the test data infers that we have a slight problem with overfitting and we may need to make some tweaks to the hyperparameters.

There are several reasons why our basic model may not guarantee exact predictions for launching a video game in the year 2017 (including the fact that the dataset is based on the last 37 years), but this is an escapable problem of predicting the future. We can, however, attempt to minimize the problem by perhaps removing rows from the dataset that contain video games produced in the 20th Century and focus on more recent trends. Deciding what information to include in our model will depend on our business context and goals. If our hypothetical video game targets families (including parents), then perhaps video games released in the 1980's are relevant to the target customer group and should be included in the model.

Secondly, the model was created on the assumption that sales in North America are not dependent on those in other regions. However, it might be possible that video game sales in markets outside of North America boost the global brand and lead to higher sales in North America. In this case, excluding total sales in Japan, Europe, and Other Regions in our model may have undermined the accuracy of the sales figure we used for North America. These are the sorts of questions you need to ask and be aware of when creating your own prediction model.

Thirdly, please take into account that because the training and test data are shuffled randomly in this model, your own exact results are bound to differ slightly when replicating this model on your own machine.

Finally, if you wish to use a different supervised machine learning algorithm and not gradient boosting, much of the code used in this exercise can be replicated. For instance, the same code can be used to import a new dataset, remove features (columns), remove rows, split and shuffle the dataset, and evaluate mean absolute error.

http://scikit-learn.org is a great resource to learn more about other algorithms as well as gradient boosting as used in this exercise.

For a copy of the code, please contact the author at oliver.theobald@contentin.asia or see the code example below. In addition, if you have troubles implementing the model using the code found in this book, please feel free to contact the author by email for extra assistance at no cost.

Code for Video Game Global Sales Model

```
# Import libraries

import pandas as pd
```

```python
from sklearn.model_selection import train_test_split

from sklearn import ensemble

from sklearn.metrics import mean_absolute_error

from sklearn.externals import joblib


# Read in data from CSV

df = pd.read_csv('~/Downloads/Video_Game_Sales_as_of_Jan_2017.csv')


# Delete unneeded columns

del df['Name']

del df['EU_Sales']

del df['JP_Sales']

del df['Other_Sales']


# Remove rows with missing values

df.dropna(axis=0, how='any', thresh=None, subset=None,
inplace=True)


# Convert non-numerical data using one-hot encoding

features_df = pd.get_dummies(df, columns=['Platform',
'Publisher', 'Genre', 'Rating'])


# Remove global sales
```

```python
del features_df['Global_Sales']


# Create X and y arrays from the dataset

X = features_df.as_matrix()

y = df['Global_Sales'].as_matrix()


# Split data into test/train set (70/30 split) and shuffle

X_train, X_test, y_train, y_test = train_test_split(X, y,
test_size=0.3, random_state=0)


# Set up algorithm

model = ensemble.GradientBoostingRegressor(

    n_estimators=150,

    learning_rate=0.1,

    max_depth=4,

    min_samples_split=4,

    min_samples_leaf=4,

    max_features=0.5,

    loss='huber'

)


# Run model on training data

model.fit(X_train, y_train)
```

```python
# Save model to file

joblib.dump(model, 'videogames_trained_model.pkl')


# Check model accuracy

mse = mean_absolute_error(y_train, model.predict(X_train))

print ("Training Set Mean Absolute Error: %.4f" % mse)


mse = mean_absolute_error(y_test, model.predict(X_test))

print ("Test Set Mean Absolute Error: %.4f" % mse)
```

WHERE TO GO NEXT

## 18

CAREER & STUDY OPTIONS

Becoming a machine learning engineer or data scientist requires a strong cross-disciplinary education, as depicted in this diagram.

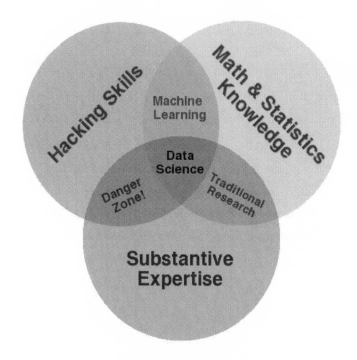

Data Science Venn Diagram, Source: http://drewconway.com

This Venn diagram was created in 2010 by Drew Conway, a well-known American data scientist and co-author of *Machine Learning for Hackers*.

With this diagram, Conway argues that data science requires a combination of three primary skills: hacking (coding), substantive expertise, and knowledge of math & statistics. While there are also four other pockets in this Venn diagram, let's first unpack the three large circles that Conway presents.

The first large circle in data science is 'hacking skills,' which is essentially coding or expertise with a programming language—and not malicious encroachment into government data files as Conway's label might suggest. Conway's choice of words, though, does emphasize the need for developers to utilize code to 'hack' and solve unique challenges rather than relying on a cookie-cutter approach. Conway, however, emphasizes, that this does not call for an advanced background in computer science but rather consolidated expertise to manipulate text files from the command-line, an understanding of vectorized operations, and an algorithmic mindset.[5]

The second large circle is substantive expertise, which refers to expertise, experience, and understanding of the domain to which one applies their research. If you are analyzing customer segmentation for a large retail store, for example, it's important that you understand the retail industry and what factors impact customers' purchasing decisions.

---

[5] Drew Conway, *The Data Science Venn Diagram*, 2010, http://drewconway.com

The third large circle is knowledge of math and statistics, and which is the main theme of this book. Statistical-based algorithms and math provide the tools to perform heavy number crunching and to analyze data. While coding can be applied to bypass the manual process of mathematical and statistical-based equations, a basic understanding of statistics is still vital. As shown in the Venn diagram, hacking skills and domain expertise without a knowledge of math and statistics is akin to operating in a danger zone (Conway even adds an exclamation mark to emphasize this point). Conway reasons that data scientists require at least a "baseline familiarity" of statistics and mathematics in order to select and interpret appropriate algorithms to work their data.[6] Data scientists without a baseline familiarity of statistics are also vulnerable to misinterpreting probability—which is vital when searching for matches and associations in datasets.

The three other sub-elements in Conway's Venn diagram are machine learning, data science, and traditional research. Traditional research constitutes statistics and domain knowledge but not coding. This refers to researchers that apply statistical analysis in their field of expertise but who do not use heavy computer processing or big data and encompasses many researchers in academia that are yet to fully embrace technology in their research.

---

[6] Drew Conway, *The Data Science Venn Diagram*, 2010, http://drewconway.com

Next is data science, which contains all three primary elements: domain knowledge to ask the right questions to prepare data analysis, statistical knowledge to design analysis, and hacking skills to implement analysis.

The final sub-element is machine learning, which draws on statistics and coding but without substantive expertise. From Conway's Venn diagram we can infer that machine learning is 50% hacking (programming) and 50% mathematics and statistics. This underlines the importance of mathematics and statistics in machine learning. This is also a key reason why I've focused the book on the same topic. However, I do want to add that substantive expertise is partially relevant to machine learning as it will help direct your analysis and guide how you configure certain algorithms. For example, if you know there to be two types of customers that buy a particular product, then you can set your k-means clustering algorithm to populate two clusters for the purpose of analysis, rather than guessing and setting your hyperparameters to a much higher number, such as 12 clusters. Admittedly, this saves time more than anything else as there are coding and statistical measures available to strike an optimal number of clusters. Nonetheless, domain knowledge does play a helpful, if albeit minor, role in the field of machine learning.

The Future of Jobs

As machine learning continues to filter into various industries, many traditional jobs are expected to become semi-automated in the near future. The integration of artificial intelligence into self-driving vehicles, surgery, and medical diagnosis is already on the cusp of replacing a large number of jobs in transportation and medical care.

Even in creative industries such as graphics and web design, AI is taking steps to replace human talent. Grid.io, for example, offers a self-standing website created solely through AI. Wix has also rolled out an AI-powered option to build and design a website based on the content of your site. In art and music, machine-generated pieces are narrowing the gap with that of human artists.

The BBC recently launched an online resource titled, "Will a robot take my job?" From this resource, you can investigate how secure your job will be in the year 2035. Research indicates that nursing jobs, for example, are protected from potential automation as the job role depends on mobility and personal interaction in a highly unpredictable work environment. Other AI resilient job roles include sales manager, hotel manager, and fitness instructor.

Conversely, common job roles including bartender, factory worker, waiter/waitress, chartered accountant, driver, and journalist face a high threat of automation. In journalism, we are already witnessing growing instances of machine-generated news in finance and sports through the timely analysis of data.

Senior managers are less at risk from the threat of automation but, their job requirements are expected to change. Linda Burch from the executive recruitment agency Burch Works states that, "Within 10 years, if you're not a data geek, you can forget about being in the C-suite."[7]

I don't entirely accept that CEOs will need to be 'data geeks,' especially in regards to technical expertise. However, I do agree that decision-makers should, at the very least, have a basic understanding of data science and an ability to understand its benefits and leverage its potential.

The speed at which machine learning is seeping into all aspects of modern work—from marketing to human resources—underscores data literacy as a key skill set for a modern workforce. Also, just as the Internet Age triggered an avalanche of new job titles, so too will the data-driven era that we're now entering.

During the formative years of the Dot-com evolution, many traditional job opportunities—including travel agent, journalist, courier, stockbroker, and Encyclopaedia salesperson—contracted or were phased out entirely. Those losses, though, were gradually filled with the creation of new job roles. An explosion of highly skilled jobs ensued in web development, search engine

---

[7] Todd Wasserman, *So you wanna be a data scientist? A guide to 2015's hottest profession,* 2014, www.mashable.com

optimization, e-commerce, online customer service, web design, affiliate marketing, and eventually social media and mobile web design. While it's possible that a high proportion of these jobs will be phased out by new breakthroughs in machine learning, new job roles will again be created.

Similarly, new employment opportunities in the AI era will demand a higher level of training and expertise. According to certain industry experts, one of the biggest inhibitors to the future development of machine learning is the present shortage of professionals with the right expertise and training.

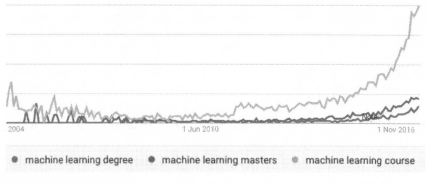

● machine learning degree ● machine learning masters ● machine learning course

Source: Google Trends

But awareness and interest in machine learning and AI career paths is growing quickly. This has triggered a positive inflection point in the total volume of Google searches related to machine learning degrees and courses over the last two years.

Education

To work in the field of machine learning, you will need passion and dedication to learn and acquire the necessary skills. There are various channels available to gain an education in machine learning. A university degree, an online degree program or an open online course, serve as three popular entry points.

Along the way, it is important to seek out mentors that you can turn to for advice on both technical questions and career options. A mentor could be a professor, a colleague, or even someone on the Internet you've never met before. If you are looking to meet data scientists and machine learning engineers with more industry-specific experience, it is recommended that you attend industry conferences or smaller offline events held in your local area, such as meetups (www.meetups.com). If you can't afford to join as a participant, there may be an option to join as a volunteer. Volunteering will not only save you money on admission fees but may, in fact, offer more access to people you wish to meet.

LinkedIn and Twitter are terrific online resources to identify professionals in the field or access leading industry voices. When reaching out to established professionals you may receive resistance or a lack of response depending on whom you are contacting. One way to overcome this potential problem is to offer your services in lieu of mentoring. For example, if you have experience and expertise in managing a WordPress website you could offer your time to build or manage an existing website for the person you are seeking to form a relationship. Other services you can offer are proofreading books, papers, and blogs, or interning at their particular company or institute. Sometimes it's best to start your search for mentors locally as that will create more opportunities to meet in person and to find local internship and job opportunities.

For technical questions, you will also definitely want to join kaggle.com, which provides an open platform to ask questions and discuss publicly available datasets.

Massive Open Online Learning

The online world is abuzz with massive open online courses (MOOC), and machine learning is one of the most popular subjects in this new learning space.

Three popular online platforms for studying machine learning are Udacity, Udemy, and Coursera. Udemy offers regular discounts and their courses tend to be highly practical and useful. However, Udacity and Coursera are generally cited as more rigorous and respected in regards to certification.

The Coursera platform provides a rich repository of video-based courses that cover a range of machine learning topics, including introductory to advanced courses, recommender systems, natural language processing, and deep learning. Coursera Co-founder and Stanford Associate Professor Andrew Ng's Machine Learning course (www.coursera.org/learn/machine-learning) is virtually a rite of passage for anyone taking their first steps in the field of machine learning.

Coursera courses, including the Andrew Ng course, are self-paced and many of these courses can be taken online free of cost. To gain official certification, students must enroll in the paid version of the course, but even then it's still relatively affordable. The cost per course is usually between USD $100-200 or USD $49 per month for membership access to 2,000 Coursera courses.

Udacity offers free stand-alone courses as well but goes a step further by offering more rigorous nano-degrees. For its nano-degree stream, Udacity has partnered with major tech companies including Facebook, Google, and IBM to shape its curriculum and case studies. Udacity's nano-degrees are priced higher than other open online courses and demand a higher level of financial and personal commitment.

At the time of writing, Udacity offers the following nano-degrees:

Machine Learning Engineer, co-created by Kaggle—6 months, $199/month. This program provides a guaranteed or money-back employment track with tech company Paysa ($299/month). Paysa is a platform for individuals to benchmark their salary and value in the job market. A base salary working as a machine learning engineer with Paysa apparently ranges from $38,400-$231,000 a year.

Artificial Intelligence, co-created by IBM Watson, Amazon

Echo and DiDi (the Chinese equivalent of Uber)—6 months, $1,600 in total. This course has a selective entry policy, accepting approximately 20-30% of all applicants.

Data Analyst, co-created by MongoDB and Facebook—12 months, $199/month or $299/month. The program also offers a guaranteed or money-back employment track with tech company Paysa.

Deep Learning Foundation, co-created by Sirag Raval of YouTube fame—17 weeks, $599-$800 in total.

For courses charged on a monthly basis, you can apply for a partial refund if you complete the course in less than the prescribed time. Udacity also offers a 7-14 day free trial, which I recommend you take up before purchasing. Finally, check the eligibility requirements for certain courses, which may request foundation to intermediate knowledge of Python and statistics.

While online courses offer flexibility, low barriers to entry and an affordable price tag, university degrees certainly maintain the mantle as the most respected form of qualification from the perspective of employers. Although perceptions are changing, traditional college degrees are respected for their competitive selection policy and rigorous curriculum. Moreover, degree programs demand a greater investment of time and money on the part of the student. As such, open online courses are not yet considered as a direct substitute for a university degree. That said, demonstrating the self-discipline to complete an open online learning course is highly respected by employers, particularly in Western countries.

If you can build a portfolio of practical projects through MOOC courses (i.e. Udacity), and contribute to online projects or participate in competitions (i.e. kaggle.com) then the open online learning option can certainly boost your employability. Hands-on experience is vital in any industry and especially for machine learning.

Degree Programs

Despite the popular uptake of on-demand education, degree programs—offline and online—remain the most effective route to gaining initial employment in the field of machine learning. In East Asia, where I work, traditional degrees remain the only currency to validate your qualifications.

Machine learning is taught in a range of degrees including data science, computer science, and artificial intelligence. However, a Master's degree in Artificial Intelligence is inherently broad and not necessarily the most direct route to finding employment in the field of machine learning. AI encompasses a wide range of sub-fields and disciplines, and machine learning may only constitute one portion of the program. A Master's degree in Artificial Intelligence is more commonly leveraged as a stepping-stone to a PhD program.

Highly respected Master's programs in machine learning are

offered at Stanford, Berkeley, Carnegie Mellon, Columbia, University of Washington, and MIT. Other reputable institutes include Edinburgh, Duke, Michigan, University of Pennsylvania, Toronto, UCSD, Brown, UCL, Georgia Tech, Cambridge, Oxford, and Cornell. Many of these colleges offer online degrees that can be taken outside of the United States.

Grad school naturally attracts a hefty price tag. There is, though, an anomaly to be found with the Online Master's of Science in Computer Science (OMS CS) offered by the Georgia Institute of Technology (www.omscs.gatech.edu) in conjunction with Udacity and AT&T. Tuition fees for the entire program are just USD $7,000! This is considerably more affordable than comparable degree programs offered in the U.S. This massive open online course is the first accredited Master's of Science in Computer Science from a traditional university and has been running since 2014.

Georgia Tech also offers an Online Master's of Science in Analytics with another mass online open course platform called edX. The program costs just under USD $10,000 for a one-year full-time degree or a two-year part-time degree.

After completing a Master's degree in machine learning/artificial intelligence/data science, there is then the option of completing a PhD in machine learning. This is an ideal route for those wishing to delve deeper into interesting topics.

PhD's in many countries are supported by government or

university funding. There is, though, a sizeable opportunity cost of completing a four-year PhD on a basic salary/stipend over working in industry on a full-time salary. In places like the United States, you can expect to receive USD $30,000 a year to complete a PhD course, compared to earning an annual salary of USD $80,000-110,000 working for a private company.

However, according to a 2017 report published by LinkedIn, *Survey of the Global AI Talent Scene* (published in Chinese), 26.7% of professionals in the U.S. currently working in AI previously worked in higher education or a research center.[8]

Google, Facebook, and Microsoft have also been known for raiding the ranks of academia to recruit talent in the space of artificial intelligence and to secure a pipeline of young talent. The prevailing logic is that hiring professors unlocks a new network of talent and makes it easier to hire former PhD students.

Finally, the other upside of completing a PhD is that you have greater control over the scope of your work and research, and the academic path overall may be a more attractive proposition for certain people.

---

[8] LinkedIn China, *Survey of the Global AI Talent Scene,* 2017, www.linkedin.cn

BUG BOUNTY

Thank you for reading this absolute beginners' introduction to machine learning. While not customary practice in the publishing industry, we offer a financial reward to readers for locating errors or bugs in this book.

For this genre of writing—statistical-based data modeling—it is not uncommon for errors to emerge in the eye of the beholder. In other words, it's natural for readers to occasionally misinterpret diagrams, copy code incorrectly or misread important concepts. This is human nature, but to avoid readers attacking the author with a one-star review and affecting future sales of this title, we invite you to report any bugs by first sending us an email at **oliver.theobald@contentin.asia**

This way we can supply further explanations and examples over email to calibrate your understanding, or in cases where you're right and we're wrong, we offer a monetary reward of USD $20. This way you can make a tidy profit from your feedback and we can update the book to improve the standard of content for all readers.

FURTHER RESOURCES

This section lists relevant learning materials for readers that wish to progress further in the field of machine learning. Please note that certain details listed in this section, including prices, may be subject to change in the future.

| Machine Learning |

Machine Learning

Format: Coursera course

Presenter: Andrew Ng

Cost: Free

Suggested Audience: Beginners (especially those with a preference for MATLAB)

A free and well-taught introduction from Andrew Ng, one of the most influential figures in this field. This course has become a virtual rite of passage for anyone interested in machine learning.

Project 3: Reinforcement Learning

Format: Online blog tutorial

Author: EECS Berkeley

Suggested Audience: Upper intermediate to advanced

A practical demonstration of reinforcement learning, and Q-learning specifically, explained through the game Pac-Man.

| Basic Algorithms |

Machine Learning With Random Forests And Decision Trees: A Visual Guide For Beginners

Format: E-book

Author: Scott Hartshorn

Suggested Audience: Established beginners

A short, affordable (USD $3.20), and engaging read on decision trees and random forests with detailed visual examples, useful practical tips, and clear instructions.

Linear Regression And Correlation: A Beginner's Guide

Format: E-book

Author: Scott Hartshorn

Suggested Audience: All

A well-explained and affordable (USD $3.20) introduction to linear regression, as well as correlation.

| The Future of AI |

The Inevitable: Understanding the 12 Technological Forces That Will Shape Our Future

Format: E-Book, Book, Audiobook

Author: Kevin Kelly

Suggested Audience: All (with an interest in the future)

A well-researched look into the future with a major focus on AI and machine learning by The New York Times Best Seller Kevin Kelly. Provides a guide to twelve technological imperatives that will shape the next thirty years.

Homo Deus: A Brief History of Tomorrow

Format: E-Book, Book, Audiobook

Author: Yuval Noah Harari

Suggested Audience: All (with an interest in the future)

As a follow-up title to the success of *Sapiens: A Brief History of Mankind,* Yuval Noah Harari examines the possibilities of the future with notable sections of the book examining machine consciousness, applications in AI, and the immense power of data and algorithms.

| Programming |

Learning Python, 5th Edition

Format: E-Book, Book

Author: Mark Lutz

Suggested Audience: All (with an interest in learning Python)

A comprehensive introduction to Python published by O'Reilly Media.

Hands-On Machine Learning with Scikit-Learn and TensorFlow: Concepts, Tools, and Techniques to Build Intelligent Systems

Format: E-Book, Book

Author: Aurélien Géron

Suggested Audience: All (with an interest in programming in Python, Scikit-Learn, and TensorFlow)

As a highly popular O'Reilly Media book written by machine learning consultant Aurélien Géron, this is an excellent advanced resource for anyone with a solid foundation of machine learning and computer programming.

| Recommendation Systems |

The Netflix Prize and Production Machine Learning Systems: An Insider Look

Format: Blog

Author: Mathworks

Suggested Audience: All

A very interesting blog article demonstrating how Netflix applies machine learning to form movie recommendations.

Recommender Systems

Format: Coursera course

Presenter: The University of Minnesota

Cost: Free 7-day trial or included with $49 USD Coursera subscription

Suggested Audience: All

Taught by the University of Minnesota, this Coursera specialization covers fundamental recommender system techniques including content-based and collaborative filtering as well as non-personalized and project-association recommender systems.

| Deep Learning |

Deep Learning Simplified

Format: Blog

Channel: DeepLearning.TV

Suggested Audience: All

A short video series to get you up to speed with deep learning. Available for free on YouTube.

Deep Learning Specialization: Master Deep Learning, and Break into AI

Format: Coursera course

Presenter: deeplearning.ai and NVIDIA

Cost: Free 7-day trial or included with $49 USD Coursera subscription

Suggested Audience: Intermediate to advanced (with experience in Python)

A robust curriculum for those wishing to learn how to build neural networks in Python and TensorFlow, as well as career advice, and how deep learning theory applies to industry.

Deep Learning Nanodegree

Format: Udacity course

Presenter: Udacity

Cost: $599 USD

Suggested Audience: Upper beginner to advanced, with basic experience in Python

Comprehensive and practical introduction to convolutional neural networks, recurrent neural networks, and deep reinforcement learning taught online over a four-month period. Practical components include building a dog breed classifier, generating TV scripts, generating faces, and teaching a quadcopter how to fly.

| Future Careers |

Will a Robot Take My Job?

Format: Online article

Author: The BBC

Suggested Audience: All

Check how safe your job is in the AI era leading up to the year 2035.

So You Wanna Be a Data Scientist? A Guide to 2015's Hottest Profession

Format: Blog

Author: Todd Wasserman

Suggested Audience: All

Excellent insight into becoming a data scientist.

The Data Science Venn Diagram

Format: Blog

Author: Drew Conway

Suggested Audience: All

The popular 2010 data science diagram designed by Drew Conway.

DOWNLOADING DATASETS

Before you can start practicing machine learning algorithms and building your first machine learning model, you will need data at your disposal. For beginners starting out in machine learning, there are a number of options. One is to source your own dataset by writing a web crawler in Python or utilizing a click-and-drag tool such as Import.io to crawl the Internet. However, the easiest and best option to get started is by visiting kaggle.com.

Kaggle is an open online community for data scientists and statisticians to access datasets, join competitions, and simply hang out and talk about data. Kaggle is therefore an ideal platform to develop your experience and credentials through active participation in competitions and other online activities.

Another great thing about Kaggle is the access to free downloadable datasets, as referenced in this book. This saves you the time and effort of sourcing and formatting your own dataset. Meanwhile, you also have the opportunity to discuss and problem-solve with other users on the forum.

Bear in mind, however, that datasets you download from Kaggle will inherently need some refining (through scrubbing) to tailor to the machine learning model that you wish to develop.

Included, as follows, are four free sample datasets from Kaggle that may prove useful to your further learning.

Starbucks Locations Worldwide

Want to know which country has the highest density of Starbucks stores, or do you want to find the most isolated Starbucks store on the planet? If yes, this is the dataset for you. Scraped from the Starbucks store location web page, this dataset includes the name and location of every Starbucks store in operation as of February 2017.

European Football Database

Sometimes not a lot happens in 90 minutes, but with 25,000+ matches and 10,000+ players over 11 leading European country championships from seasons 2008 to 2016, this is the dataset for football/soccer diehards.

The dataset even includes team lineups with squad formation represented in x, y coordinates, betting odds from 10 providers, and detailed match events including goals, possession, goals, cards, and corners.

New York Stock Exchange

Interested in fundamental and technical analysis? With up to 30% of stock transactions said to be machine generated, can this number go higher based on lessons learned from historical data?

This dataset includes prices, fundamentals, and securities retrieved from Yahoo Finance, Nasdaq Financials, and EDGAR

SEC databases. From this dataset you can examine what impacts ROI and what indicates future bankruptcy.

Brazil's House of Deputies Reimbursements

As politicians in Brazil are entitled to receive refunds from money spent on activities that 'better serve the people,' there are interesting findings and suspicious outliers to be found from this dataset.

Data regarding these expenses are publicly available, but there is still very little monitoring of expenses in Brazil. So don't be surprised to see one public servant racking up over 800 flights in twelve months, and another that recorded R$140,000 (USD $44,500) on postal expenses—yes, snail mail!

FINAL WORD

Now has never been a better time to study machine learning and I strongly recommend you sign up to the free Andrew Ng course on Coursera to further develop your understanding of machine learning.

Also, if you haven't started already, another important next step is to learn a programming language such as Python. You can start by joining a programming course on Udemy, Lynda, or Code Academy. Books are a wonderful resource, but sometimes video format makes it that little bit easier to digest and see a programming language in practice.

Despite the rigorous training ahead, you can feel confident that you're moving into a hot job market with many big business, social, and global problems to solve.

I sincerely wish you all the best with your future career in machine learning. If you have any direct feedback, both positive and negative, or suggestions, please feel free to write to me at oliver.theobald@contentin.asia where I will look forward to hearing from you.

Please also note that under Amazon's Matchbook program, the purchaser of this book can add the Kindle version of this title (valued at $3.99 USD) to their Amazon Kindle library at no cost.

Finally, I would like to express my gratitude to my colleagues Jeremy Pederson and Rui Xiong for their assistance in kindly sharing practical machine learning tips and some sections of code used in this book.